Skiathos
a Greek Island Paradise
3rd Edition

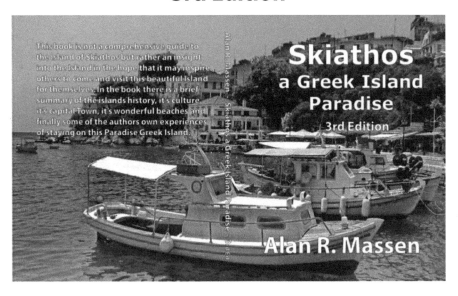

This book is not intended to be a comprehensive guide to the Island of Skiathos but rather an insight into the Island in the hope that it may inspire others to come and visit this beautiful Island for themselves. In the book there is a brief summary of the islands history, it's culture, it's capital Town, it's wonderful beaches and finally some of the authors own experiences of staying on this Paradise Greek Island.

The Greek flag and Alan on Skiathos

by Norfolk Watercolour Artist - Alan R. Massen
Published in Great Britain by Rainbow Publications UK

Books by the same Author

Retiring to the Garden Year 1 - Paperback
Retiring into a Rainbow- Paperback and Hardback
Retiring into a Rainbow - 1st Edition - My Favourite Artwork 2020 - 1st Edition
Retiring to our Garden Year one - 1st & 2nd Editions
Retiring to our Garden Year two - 1st & 2nd & 3rd Editions
Retiring into a Rainbow - 1st & 2nd Editions
Skiathos a Greek Island Paradise - 1st & 2nd & 3rd Editions
Norfolk the County of my Birth - 1st & 2nd & 3rd Editions
Art Inspired by a Rainbow - 1st & 2nd & 3rd & 4th Editions
Ibiza Island of Dreams - 1st & 2nd Editions
Majorca Island in the Sun - 1st & 2nd Editions
Flip-Flops and Shades on Thassos - 1st & 2nd & 3rd Editions
Mardle and a Troshin' in Norfolk - 1st & 2nd Editions
England the Country of my Birth - 1st & 2nd Editions
Mousehole the Cornish Jewel - 1st & 2nd & 3rd Editions
Sunshades & Flip-Flops on Kefalonia - 1st & 2nd & 3rd Editions
Shades & Flip-Flops on Zakynthos - 1st & 2nd & 3rd Editions
Trips into my Minds Eye - 1st & 2nd & 3rd & 4th Editions
Corfu and Mainland Greece - 1st & 2nd & 3rd Editions
Crete and the Island of Santorini - 1st & 2nd & 3rd Editions
Cyprus - Pyramids - Holy Land - 1st & 2nd & 3rd Editions
Greek Islands in the Sun - 1st & 2nd & 3rd Editions
Being Greek - 1st & 2nd & 3rd Editions

E-books and Booklets:

Retiring to the Garden Yr 1 - Retiring into a Rainbow - My Art 1997 - 2018 - Skiathos a Greek Paradise Island
My Norfolk - My Greece - My England - My Team - My Skiathos - My Art - My Album of Visual Art
My Village - Greece Land of Gods and Men - Norfolk Wildlife - Civilisation (Empires of the Past)
Boudica Queen of the Iceni - Roman Britain

Alan on Skiathos…

First Published in 2015 by Rainbow Publications UK
2nd Edition Published in 2019 by Rainbow Publications UK
3rd Edition Published in 2020 by Rainbow Publications UK

Paperback Edition ISBN 978-0-9933962-3-6

Typeset in Minion Pro

Published in Great Britain by Rainbow Publications UK

Dedication

Welcome to my book called **"Skiathos a Greek Island Paradise".** I would like to dedicate this book to all those people worldwide who have lost loved ones during the recent terrible Coronavirus pandemic of 2020. All those who have left us will always be remembered and live on in our hearts and minds as we remember all of the love, support and smiles that they shared with us during their lifetimes. I would also like to thank the wonderful, dedicated and brave doctors, nurses and all of the other essential workers who put their own lives at risk to help others during this tragedy. Their bravery has been an inspiration to us all during this awful time and we thank each and to every one of them. **THANK YOU**…

I would also like to dedicate this the 54th book that I have had published to my orthopaedic surgeon Mr. James Jeffery, all the members of my family and all of our friends. A special mention must also go to Evia, and George of the Mythos Cafe in the Old Port Skiathos Town, George, Yellis, Katherine, Alexei, Yannis, Katia, Yannis, Ervin, Dori, Tim, Michel and Vangelis and everyone else at the Troulos Bay Hotel on the paradise Greek Island of Skiathos and to our good friends Karl, Anna, Issy, Alistair, Andrew and Lynn. A special thank you to my lovely wife Susie who accompanies me on all of life journeys. Last, but not lest, to all of the wonderful people of Greece that we have met over the years whilst visiting their beautiful Country.

by Norfolk watercolour artist - Alan R. Massen.
Published by Rainbow Publications UK

About the Author

Susie and Alan at the Troulos Bay Hotel on Skiathos

Alan was born in the city of Norwich in the county of Norfolk, England in November 1949. When Alan was still a teenager he started painting whilst attending art classes in Norwich. In his mid-teens he had two paintings accepted for a National Art Exhibition held in London and other major UK cities. Alan spent most of his working life as a professional Health and Safety Advisor and rarely picked up a paint brush until Alan, his wife Susie and daughter Ginny (his other daughter Mandy is married and lives with her husband Adrian in Sheffield) moved out of the city of Norwich into the countryside in 1993. They moved to a little village called East Lexham in the heart of Norfolk. The village was very peaceful and pretty. This helped inspire Alan to take up watercolour painting once again. In 2004 they moved to another small West Norfolk village near Downham Market where they still live today. In 2008 Alan had to retire due to ill health (bad knees) and whilst he still painted regularly he began to spend more and more time gardening. In 2013 his wife Susie suggested that he kept a gardening diary to record his adventures in the garden and capture the changing seasons, animals, birds and the successes and failures of being a gardener he encountered. By the following year Susie suggested that he should write a book from his diary and include illustrations of both the garden and his artwork. In 2014 Alan's first book was published by Creative Gateway called "Retiring to the Garden – Year One". This was follow up with his second book called "Retiring into a Rainbow" featuring his watercolour paintings. After changing his publisher to Rainbow Publications UK. Alan, by 2020, has written and had published another fifty paperback books.

Contents

The Old Port in Skiathos Town

Published in Great Britain by Rainbow Publications UK

Introduction

Skiathos Town and the Troulos Bay Hotel

The Island of Skiathos is one of the Sporades group of Greek Islands that lie just off the east coast of mainland Greece. It is the nearest Greek Island to the mainland. Skiathos has its own international airport and good ferry links to nearby Islands and to the mainland of Greece. Skiathos is Susie and my personnel favourite Island of all of the many Greek Islands. The Island was one of the first to cash in on the Greek holiday boom thanks to having it's own international airport. Skiathos has remained, over the years, one of the most popular Greek Paradise Island holiday destinations. We have holidayed at the beautiful Troulos Bay Hotel in Troulos (see above) on the Island numerous times. The Island of Skiathos is a small and compact Island, just 12 km long and about 6 km wide, and it has a plethora of large, deep, sandy beaches strung all along its southern coastline. Recent years have seen an explosion in tourist facilities and, nowadays, there is virtually an unbroken line of hotels, apartments, shops and neon-lit tavernas flanking the once rural road that runs the full length of the south coast of the Island...

Skiathos Town

The new and the old port in Skiathos Town

Skiathos Town at night is a magical place. The busy atmosphere of the day gives way to a more relaxed environment where tourists and locals alike parade up and down the promenades of the Old Port, the Bourtzi and the New Port in their best outfits or in the case of us UK visitors shorts and a brightly coloured tee shirt and sandals or flip-flops on our feet. While in Skiathos Town Susie and I love sitting in the Mythos Café in the Old Port having a drink (or two) with our friend and owner George whilst watching the World go by. We believe that it is time well spent and the friendliness of the locals is great. Or you can, if you prefer, join the throngs of holiday shoppers cruising the Skiathos Town boutiques and trinket shops that line the nearly traffic-free central shopping street…

Around the Island

Skiathos is noted among the Greek Islands for its profusion of soft sandy beaches. The whole south coast of this small Island is a succession of sandy coves. Quiet and deserted coves are few and far between, with the Kalamaki Peninsula offering the best chance of a day away from the crowds. The few north coast beaches are much more remote and have avoided the crowds because they are less easy to reach. There is a very good local bus service from Skiathos Town down the full length of the south coast of the Island. Most of the golden sandy beaches of Skiathos are strung along the Island's south coast. Well sheltered from the northerly meltemi wind, many are set in medium sized coves/bays and backed by pine draped hills. They are all serviced by the single good asphalt road that runs the length of the Island. Some beaches are backed by low rise hotels and many get very busy in the summer. Most enjoy deep sand, shallow seas with all the usual tourist facilities. So let us begin our journey together around the Island of Skiathos…

Around the Island

The beaches of Xanemos and Megali Ammos

Xanemos is one of the Island's naturist beaches and it is found at the end of the airport runway near Skiathos town. It can get very windy here and there is not much in the way of shelter. Xanemos beach is deep and flat but with more shingle than sand. A cantina opens in the summer with a dozen or so sunbeds for hire. Nevertheless, Xanemos is easily reached from Skiathos Town by bus or taxi or even on foot around the eastern end of the Island. The village of Kalyvia is nearby, a pretty spot in the hills above Xanemos on the road to the Evangelistra monastery. It is isolated with no bus service and a long and steep walk to Skiathos Town. Another beach within walking distance of Skiathos town (but in the opposite direction) is **Megali Ammos**; a mixture of sand and shingle that slopes gently into the sea and makes up part of the same beach as neighbouring **Vassilias**. The name Megali Ammos means 'large sands', although the beach is quite narrow, especially when covered in sunbeds. The road to the beach is steep but the hill behind does offer protection from northerly winds. The pretty waterfront is lined with tavernas and cafes and there is a small quay for fishing boats. Inland are several more tourist shops, cafes and a clutch of bars…

Around the Island

Buckets and spades on Vassilias beach

For walkers there is a road to the right of Villa Ella in **Megali Ammos** that peters out into an old coastal footpath leading to **Katsarou, Platanias, Kolios, Livetakia** and **Kechria**. The narrow sand and pebble beach at **Vassilias** (it translates as the King's beach') lies west of Skiathos Town and is an extension of the busier and more popular **Megali Ammos** beach. The best of the sand is at the eastern end of the beach where there are sunbeds and plenty of natural shade from the trees that border the back of the beach. **Vassilias** sits below steep hills that protects the beach from northerly winds. At the western end it is hardly a beach at all actually, just a very narrow strip of sand and rocks hugging the steep cliffs that rise almost vertically behind and a steep road that winds down to the shore past a small taverna…

Around the Island

Views of Achladies beach

South-west of the resorts of **Megali Ammos** and **Vassilias** is the coastal village of **Katsarou**. **Katsarou** is a typical Greek sleepy village of cobbled streets and whitewashed houses just above the main road on the steep pine-carpeted hillside. The elevated position makes it cooler but the relative isolation will not suit everyone. It is a steep one kilometre walk downhill to the beaches at **Vassilias** and **Kassandra Bay**. There are a couple of pleasant tavernas in the village. **Achladies**, or **Achlaidies**, is not the easiest beach to find, unless you are a resident of the large Espirides hotel that backs onto the sands and pretty much monopolises the shore. To get to the beach there is a steep track to the east or some zig-zag steps through an apartment complex. An alternative is to walk through the hotel itself or to take a fenced concrete path to the west that leads through a friendly taverna. **Achladies** beach (the name means 'Pear Trees') is long and narrow but the sand is very fine and the sea water is shallow. Tavernas at the western end provide good food and a romantic setting. The beach is set at the end of a small valley floor, planted out with olives and citrus trees. There are views from **Achladies** beach to the Islet of **Tsougria** offshore and on the horizon you can just make out the **Island of Skopelos**. More tavernas and mini markets are up on the main road just above the beach…

Around the Island

Views of Tzaneria beach

The small and sometimes heavily crowded, **Tzaneria** beach is the 'gateway' to the **Kalamaki peninsular** and dominated by the huge Nostos hotel complex whose apartment blocks climb up the nearby hillside. **Tzaneria** beach is not very wide but it is deep and the fine sand is regularly raked flat by staff from the hotel. Sheltered by cliffs, the seawater here is often mill pond still. A small taverna backs onto the beach and nearby woods offer shade along the edge of the sand. For the more sporty visitors there is a scuba diving school on the beach. Nearby, down a dirt track from bus stop 11 is the small and delightful beach of **Sklithri**, hemmed in by hills and with a small traditional taverna. The small bay provides very good shelter for boats. The pine cloaked **Kalamaki peninsula** juts out into the sea between the resorts of **Tzanaries** and **Kolios**. **Kalamaki** remains one of the more exclusive areas on the Island of Skiathos, dotted with up-market homes and apartments. The area is also noted for its walking trails through the pines with fine sea views especially between **Tzanaries** and **Kanapitsa**. The road from Bus stop 12 to 13 goes right around the peninsula. Beaches in the small bays around the **Kalamaki** coast may not be the most spectacular and are not easily reaches but they benefit as a result by being far less crowded…

Around the Island

The beach at Kanapitsa and the water taxi going into old port

The main beach resort on the **Kalamaki peninsula** is at **Kanapitsa** which has two stretches of beach, both long and narrow but very sandy and with shallow seawater. A large beach taverna provides refreshments and there is an **hourly water taxi service to Skiathos Town** which is a 20-minute journey and leaves from the jetty on the beach. There are many small coves around the coast of **Kalamaki**. Half-way around the peninsula and down a very steep footpath, is the small beach of **Koutsouri**. Around some rocks at **Koutsouri** brings you to the tiny but beautiful beach of **Delfiniki** which translates as 'Little Dolphin'. It can be reached from the road but it is a difficult scramble so most arrive on the beach by boat. The western side of the **Kalamaki peninsula** tends to be hotter, away from the prevailing northeast breeze, but there are spectacular views across the sea to the Greek **Island of Evia** and to the Greek mainland beyond to enjoy. The beach at **Vromolimnos** is very popular with young people thanks largely to a beach bar that blasts out loud music all day long and even throws the occasional foam party on the sands. It has all the usual watersports and plenty of beach facilities for the young but, as the sands are both popular and narrow, it may feel claustrophobic at busy times of the day. **Vromolimnos** is a splendid beach with powder-puff sand and some pleasant swimming in the shallow seawater and is an ideal spot for children. Being west facing, the beach both escapes the prevailing north-east winds and offers some very fine sunsets…

Around the Island

The beach at Kolios and a local fishing boat

The resort of **Kolios** sits in a small and attractive bay and has a narrow beach of sharp sand. Boats regularly tie up to the small jetty and there is a pleasant and shady taverna up some steps at the back of the sands. It is a popular destination, both for beach visitors and day trip boats, **Kolios** beach can get crowded in the high season. Most of the time though **Kolios** is pleasantly low-key. The sands shelve gently and there is good swimming to be had, making this a fine beach for families with children. There are tree-covered headlands both west and east that also helps make this a sheltered spot. A short walk in either direction reveals many small and attractive coves where the lucky ones can end up with their own 'private' beach all day. The large valley at **Platanias** is about six kilometres from Skiathos Town and has a pleasant freshwater stream that runs throughout the year. Several tavernas and snack bars have been added to accommodate the annual influx of visitors. The long and sandy **Platanias** beach (also called **Agia Paraskevi**) has a couple of beach tavernas that open in the summer. The beach lies in the same large bay as the beaches at both **Vromolimnos** and **Kolios**. The sand at **Agia Paraskevi** is fine and soft but does shelve quite steeply into the seawater so it is not ideal for families with young children. The beach has a range of watersports on offer as well as boats for hire. There are several good walks in the area, the most notable is from bus stop 16 towards **Kechria** beach, with an abandoned monastery on the way, or alternatively a right turn takes walkers over the hills back to Skiathos Town…

Around the Island

Shades on Troulos Bay beach and the Troulos Bay Hotel

The big, sandy beach at **Troulos Bay** is a very popular holiday centre and has plenty of tourist facilities, including a couple of decent tavernas and a very good small hotel called the Troulos Bay Hotel that is right on the beach. We stay at this hotel every time we have holidayed on the Island. The wide sands at Troulos Bay (the name means "Dome' in Greek and there is a dome-shaped Islet offshore) leaves plenty of room for everyone. There are some low dunes at the back of the beach. There is also a fresh water river that flows down to the beach that has terrapins and fish in that the many visitors like to feed. There are lots of sunbeds and umbrellas on the beach and the sand slopes gently into the seawater. Being south facing the beach can get very hot at mid-day but there are several good tavernas that offer good shade and food so you can escape the heat and have a great meal. The Troulos Bay Hotel also has a fine restaurant and several good lunchtime snack bars so you can also enjoy a lunch or evening meal accompanied by a great sea view. There are secluded coves along the coast for those who are prepared to explore the wooded headland, but the going can be difficult on foot and it may be better to hire one of the boats that are available on the beach if you want to explore these…

Around the Island

Views of Troulos Bay and of the village of Troulos crossroads

The **Troulos village** resort is some way inland, and purpose-built for the tourist trade. Visitors based here face a long trek to the sea, although new apartments are being built nearer to **Troulos Bay** beach every year. The village of Troulos itself is located inland on the coast road and has supermarkets, car hire, petrol station and some very good tavernas. There is also a well known dog shelter located near the monastery inland above the village and the dogs there love being taken for a walk so if you fancy something different to do during your holiday this could be for you. Either as you walk the dog or just take yourself out for a walk you can head off right from the village centre crossroads, passing the dog shelter, before heading down the dirt tracks that go to the northern beach at **Asselinos**, passing the **Kounistra Monastery** on the way. The resort of **Troulos Bay** offers not just the sea, sand and sunshine but lovely walks and great views as well…

Around the Island

View of Maratha and Koukounaries beaches and boats sailing by

The secluded bay at **Maratha** lies below the Skiathos Palace hotel just beyond the beach resort of **Koukounaries** and has virtually been commandeered by the hotel. However, it is just a short walk down from the local bus stop to the small sandy bay, well protected beneath pine covered slopes where trees reach right down to the shore. There are sunbeds and a good beach taverna in the woods behind the beach. The seawater at **Maratha** is quite shallow so the beach is good for families with children and there is plenty of natural shade from the pine trees that overhang the back of the narrow beach. **Marathi** is a peaceful alternative to neighbouring **Koukounaries** which tends to attract the big crowds, especially in the high season…

Around the Island

Koukounaries beach and small harbour

Koukounaries is regularly voted one of the top ten beaches in the world, it boasts a kilometre-long sickle of golden sand backed by a wooded nature reserve and a large lagoon. Impressive at first light, the rising sun soon lures the visitors to the sunbeds and the sea is littered with motorboats and the air is humming to the whine of jet skis. The resorts nature reserve status of its lagoon has helped curb tourist development and there are just a couple of beach tavernas. The sands are also overlooked by two hotels. The nearby lagoon is a haven for mosquitoes and virulent squadrons of wasps regularly patrol the overflowing waste bins. That said, **Koukounaries** is still a spectacular beach. The deep long sands and shallow seawater will appeal to families and there are some lovely walks in the surrounding woodland. Three watersports centres offer all manner of fun and there are toilets and changing facilities nearby. There is also an attractive small harbour at the eastern end of the beach. Large crowds cluster for a teatime scramble aboard the half-hourly local buses back to Skiathos Town and no quarter is given as homebound tourists elbow each other to get aboard and make a stampede for seats. Crammed to sardine-tin capacity the buses lumber away in a cloud of dust and exhaust smoke back towards Town. There is no village in **Koukounaries**, just a scattering of small scale hotels and tavernas strung along the road behind the Koukounaries lagoon, beach and fishing boat harbour. A horse riding centre is also located nearby…

Around the Island

Agia Eleni and Megas Asselinos beaches

Exposed to the often strong northerly winds, the west and north coasts of Skiathos are wilder and less accessible than the south. There are also far fewer beaches and all are more difficult to reach. Good roads lead to **Agia Eleni** in the west and to **Megas Asselinos** in the north but other beaches can only be reached by boat or on foot. Those that venture north are rewarded with less populated countryside and some wonderful walks through the pine forests. Between **Koukounaries** and **Agia Eleni** is the popular **Krassas** beach that is better known as **Banana Beach**. It is signposted from the car park at **Koukounaries** but it is quite a long trek through the woods so some prefer the water taxi from Skiathos Town. **Banana Beach** has two beaches. The main beach is deep, long, sandy and heavily decked with sunbeds with beach bars tucked away in the pine and scrub that lines the small cliff behind. The soft sand shelves steeply into the sea. **Banana Beach** is hugely popular with young people. Beach parties can erupt in high season at any time and it can get very noisy. The second beach, called **Little Banana**, lies just around a rocky headland. It is the Island's semi-official nudist beach. Small and flat, it's bound by steep, rocky cliffs that offer some privacy. There is a less well known, but equally attractive, beach nearby called **Spartacus** by tourists but also known as **Apelakia** among the Greeks. It lies further around the rocky headland…

Around the Island

Mandraki Elias and Agistri beaches

The secluded beach of **Agia Eleni** is at the western end of the Island, just a short walk from the bus stop before the **Koukounaries** car park. The road forks right over a small hill to the small bay. Two small cantinas sit of the northern end of a narrow beach of sharp sand and fine pebbles. The seawater is shallow and **Agia Eleni** is popular with families. West facing, it has great sunset views. A rough track leads around the headland to other small bays. Signs point to **Krifi Ammos** (**Hidden Beach**) a 15-minute walk takes you to a lovely cove with a sand and pebble beach. A beach cantina sits on the hillside but the drop into the seawater is very steep so it's not really suitable for children. There is also no room for turning cars so they are best left behind. The densely wooded area of **Mandraki** offers, after a 40-minute walk from **Koukounaries**, the three lovely beaches of **Xerxes**, **Elias** and **Agistri**. The beach at **Xerxes**, often referred to as Mandraki, is the furthest west and is backed by a cliff of red sandstone. It has calm, shallow seawater and sunbeds around the beach cantina. The central beach of **Elias** is long, deep and sandy and, although it drops sharply at the western end, it is far more shallow to the east where the dunes roll up behind the beach. A small cantina is sited on the edge of the wood overlooking the beach. **Elias** merges into the cove at **Agistri** or **Angistros** and there is often enough driftwood lying around for visitors to build complex and arresting sun shelters. This is a popular port of call for excursion boats but the relative isolation keeps numbers down and this north coast beach trio makes a fine alternative to the south shore beaches…

Around the Island

Views of the rock arch formation at Lalaria beach

The big, wild and windy beach at **Megas Asselinos** is the most accessible northern beach on the Island with a new road through the woods from the crossroads in the **village of Troulos**. It has a huge taverna and a large campsite nearby. In August the meltemi wind can blow your socks off. It is a huge beach with plenty of deep sand and some pebbles but there is little shade. A fork right on the approach road to **Megas Asselinos** takes you to **Mikri Asselinos**, a much smaller, much more secluded beach that is a favourite with naturists. The lovely beach at **Lalaria** is accessible only from the sea and is famed the world over for its white pebble beach, turquoise seawater and spectacular rock arches. The bleached white stones and undersea marble slabs are responsible for a dazzling aquamarine seashore. **Lalaria** beach is on the itinerary of almost every pleasure boat on the Island and scores of visitors embark in the hourly boat landings. Some boats will anchor up for two or three hours and there are no facilities on **Lalaria** Beach. It is a very pretty spot but there is nothing to do but avoid the crowds and more pleasure might be gained from the ubiquitous postcards of **Lalaria** beach that are on sale in almost every shop on the paradise Island of Skiathos. Now that we have been all the way around the coast of the island it is now time for us find out what to expect when you actually land in paradise...

Landing in Paradise

Landing in Paradise

My wife Susie and I, over the years, have been very fortunate to be able to holiday at the Troulos Bay Hotel on Skiathos many times. We have also holidayed on many of the Island that the Mediterranean has to offer. These include Thassos, Kefalonia, Corfu, Zakynthos , Ithaca, Santorini, Crete and of course Skiathos . Out of all of these it is only Skiathos that we return to time and time again. This is because we love it so much. Skiathos has friendly island people, lovely sandy beaches, warm blue seawater, great seafood and long lazy days of sunshine. What more could any discerning holiday maker want. So now you know why we holiday on Skiathos it is time to try and encourage you to experience this Greek paradise island for yourselves. So we will begin with some facts about the island of Skiathos and then I will share with you some of our memories of holidaying to this beautiful island. So with your seatbelt secure and your table in the upright position let us get ready to land and explore the Island of Skiathos…

Landing in Paradise

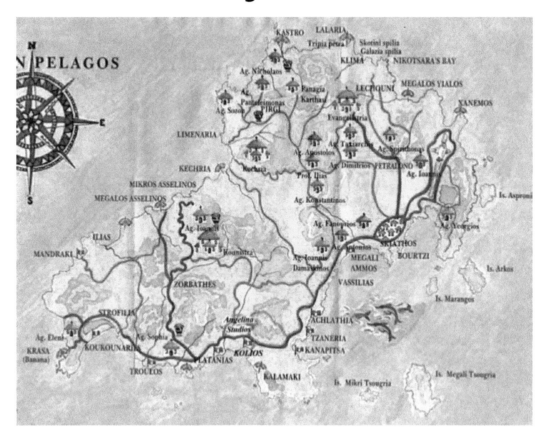

Map of the Island of Skiathos

The Island of Skiathos has a north to south western direction and is about 12 kilometres (7 miles) long and 6 kilometres (4 miles) wide on average. The coastline is indented with inlets, capes and peninsulas. The southeast and southwest parts have gentler slopes and that is where most settlements and facilities are located. The terrain is more rugged on the north coast, with the highest peak at 433 m (1,421 feet) on mount Karafiltzanaka. The main town is Skiathos and along with the airport is located to the northeast next to a lagoon. The other main settlements are: Xanemos - Kalyvia - Troulos and Koukounaries. The Municipality of Skiathos includes the islets of Tsougria, Tsougriaki, Maragos, Arkos, Troulonisi and Aspronisi. They are scattered a few kilometres off the southeast coastline and are clearly visible from the town and the beaches. The island of Skopelos is visible from Skiathos with the more distant islands of Euboea and Skyros visible under very clear weather conditions. The main paved road runs all along the south eastern stretch of the island with several narrow dirt roads branching off towards the interior and the northern coast. Farmland exists around all the major settlements on the island…

Landing in Paradise

Ancient Greek war helmet and some of the Greek Gods

A brief History of Skiathos a Greek paradise Island: Despite its small size, Skiathos with its many beaches and wooded landscape is a popular tourist destination. It has over 60, mostly sandy, beaches scattered around the 44 km (27 mile) coastline. Some of these are Troulos Bay, Vromolimnos, Koukounaries, Asselinos, Megali Ammos and Mandraki. Much of the island is wooded with Aleppo Pine and a small Stone Pine forest at Koukounaries location where there is a lagoon and a popular beach. The island's forests are concentrated on the southwest and northern parts, but the presence of pine trees is prevalent throughout the island. In ancient times, the island played a minor role during the Persian Wars. In 480 BC, the fleet of the Persian King Xerxes was hit by a storm and was badly damaged on the rocks of the Skiathos coast. Following this the Greek fleet blockaded the adjacent seas to prevent the Persians from invading the mainland and supplying provisions to the army facing the 300 Spartans defending the pass at Thermopylae. The Persian fleet was defeated there at Artemisium and finally destroyed at the Battle of Salamis a year later. Skiathos remained in the Delian League until it lost its independence. Skiathos Town was totally destroyed by Philip V of Macedon when he invaded in 200 BC…

Landing in Paradise

The Bourtzi and the church on the hill

In 1207 the Gyzi brothers captured the island and built the Bourtzi, a small Venetian-styled fortress similar to the Bourtzi in Nafplio, on an islet just out of Skiathos Town, to protect the capital from the pirates. But the Bourtzi was ineffective in protecting the population and in the mid-14th century the inhabitants moved the capital from the ancient site that lay where modern Skiathos Town is to Kastro (the Greek word for castle), located on a high rock, overlooking a steep cliff above the sea at the northernmost part of the island. In 1704 monks from Athos built the Evangelistria monastery which played a part in the Greek War of Independence as a hide-out for Greek rebels. The first flag of Greece was created and hoisted in the Evangelistria monastery on Skiathos in 1807. Several prominent military leaders (including Theodoros Kolokotronis and Andreas Miaoulis) had gathered there for consultation concerning an uprising, and they were sworn to this flag by the local bishop. After the War of Independence and demise of piracy in the Aegean, Kastro became less important as a strategic location. In 1830's, the island's capital was moved back to the original site where it still remains today...

Landing in Paradise

A day out in Skiathos Town

Today, ruins of Kastro are one of the Islands tourist attractions. During the 19th century Skiathos became an important shipbuilding centre in the Aegean due to the abundance of pine forests on the island. The pine woods of the island were then almost obliterated. This was brought to a halt though, due to the emergence of steamboats. A small shipwright remains north of Skiathos Town, which still builds traditional Greek Caiques. The film Mamma Mia was partially filmed on Skiathos and the nearby island of Skopelos. This has increased its popularity as a tourist destination since the release of the successful movie. Hollywood actor Richard Romanus moved to the island in 2001 with his wife. He has written a book about his move to the island called "Act III" and I have read it and very good it is too. Transportation to Skiathos by sea: There is a regular boat service to the island and the rest of the Sporades islands with departures from Volos and Agios Konstantinos. The boats are operated mainly by Hellenic Seaways using its high-speed Flying Cat vessel as well as conventional ferries…

Landing in Paradise

Plane arriving at Skiathos airport and the road into Town

Skiathos Islands Papadaiamandis International Airport is at the northeast of the island next to a lagoon and a lowland isthmus separating the island from the peninsula of Lazareta. Skiathos airport is served by Olympic Air flights from both Athens and Thessaloniki, while foreign airlines provide charter flights from a range of airports in European countries such as the United Kingdom, France, Austria, the Netherlands, Italy, Cyprus and Scandinavian countries. During the winter of 2013/2014, work began to expand the airport, with a runway extension, and increased the hard standing for parked aircraft. The modern major road runs along the eastern and southern coast. Narrower roads, some paved and some dirt, reach the interior and the northwest coastline. There is regular, and during tourist season, very frequent bus transit from the main town to all the resorts on the south of the island up as far as the terminus at Koukounaries beach in the southwest…

Landing in Paradise

Useful information:

Cycle, Scooter, Motor Cycle and Car hire are readily available at all resorts and in Skiathos Town. There are four petrol stations around the Town ring road and one on the main road at Troulos. The local bus is both reliable and frequent and runs to the resorts along the south coast every 15 minutes during the tourist season. Some useful bus stop resort (**numbers**) are:

- (0) - Bus station in Skiathos Town
- (1) - Supermarket
- (4) - Acropolis and medical centre
- (6) - Megali Ammos
- (7) - Mitikas (8) - Vasillias (9) - Cape Mitikas (10) - Achladias
- (12) - Nostos
- (13) - Platanias Bay /Kanapitsa
- (14) - Ag. Paraskevi
- (17) - Poros
- (18) - Troulos Village
- (20) - Troulos Bay beach
- (22) - Koukounaries Port & (25) Golden beach
- (26) - Koukounaries beach/Banana beach

Susie and I always use the local bus when we holiday on Skiathos but it is very easy to explore the island whatever your preferred form of transport may be. As the island is relatively small you can even reach the beaches on the north coast by selecting the nearest bus stop and walking over the hills if you so wish...

Landing in Paradise

Useful information:

There are three bus routes on the island. The core route (mentioned on the previous page) is from the main town to Koukounaries beach which travels along the south coast of the island. There are in total 26 bus stops, with Koukounaries Beach being the last stop, number 26 and Skiathos Town bus station being number 0. This route operates a fleet of five coaches as frequently as five times an hour during the summer peak season throughout the day, but is significantly reduced during the winter. The second route departs from Skiathos Town, to the Monastery of Evangelistria at an hourly daily schedule and the third bus route to Xanemos on the north coast with up to six round trips daily, both operated using mini-buses. Now that we know a little about the size, location, history and transport links of the Island of Skiathos I will now share with you our memories of getting on that plane from the UK and arriving for our holiday on the Greek Paradise Island of Skiathos…

Landing in Paradise

Gatwick Airport in the UK and a gull in full flight

Flying into Paradise: We have always flown with Thomson from London Gatwick on a Friday when we have gone to Skiathos. We leave our North West Norfolk home at 5 am and arrive at the airport at about 7.30 am. The first task is to report to the departure desk to get rid of our cases and get our boarding passes. The next thing we do is have a full English breakfast to set us up for the day then it's a stroll around the shops for those last minute things before going through passport control at about 11 am. Our flight leaves at 12.20 pm so we usually have a drink and get some snacks to eat on the plane then it's down to the departure gate and onto the plane. The flight takes about 3 hours and 20 minutes…

Landing in Paradise

We are
nearly there…

The Flight: We always have extra legroom seating so the flight is quite comfortable and soon it is time to look out of the window, as the wheels go down, to get our first glimpse of Skiathos. We land at about 15.40 pm UK time but it is really 17.40 pm local time. As we come into land the plane flies very low over the bay in front of Skiathos Town and the pilot comes on the intercom and tells everyone that we will hear loud engine noises as he puts the jets into full reverse as the runway is rather short (they extended the runway in 2015). As usual many of the passengers clap and cheer when we are safely down. Bless them. The pilot must get a superb view of the runway and island as he banks the aircraft ready for him/her to make the final descent. The direction we land will depend on the wind direction at the time. So we have had our onboard snacks and a couple of drinks to while away the time and maybe read our kindle and now comes one of those exciting moments that only air flight can provide the landing. I really enjoy every moment of both the takeoff and landing whenever we fly but now that we are almost back to our paradise island I hope that our two weeks do not also fly. As we zoom into land the plane wheels almost touch the people watching just outside the airport perimeter fence which is very close to the end of the runway. We have also ventured down to the end of the runway ourselves to watch other peoples plane land and it is not for the faint hearted. The loud noise and the dangerous thrust of the jet engines as the plane swoops just overhead makes this something that perhaps you should avoid or at least view from a safe distance. You can feel a sense of excitement and anticipation infect the passengers onboard who cannot wait to take that first step out of the plane into their dreams. When the plane is safely down and taxing towards the arrivals apron of the airport terminal and as usual most people are already out of their seats fighting with the overhead hand luggage compartments but for Susie and I it is different as we just sit there in our seats and enjoy the feeling of being back in our paradise island once more. The plane comes to a halt, the seat belt signs go off (already ignored by many) and it is time for that moment when you step out of the plane and into the sights, smells and heat that can only mean that you have arrived at last back in paradise…

Arriving at the Troulos Bay Hotel

The Troulos Bay Hotel on Skiathos

The Arrivals Hall: Like every other passenger we troop through passport control and into the arrivals hall (don't forget to get a copy of the free map usually available here) then it's the scrum down for the famous luggage carousel! Again we tend to sit down and wait while others try to find the optimum place around the carousel. We on the other hand over the years have learnt that sods law says that your luggage will always come around last. When we have retrieved our cases it is through the arrivals hall, out the door and after asking the Thomson representative what our coach number is we make our way outside. We always use the transfer coach provide by the tour operator because it has always proved to be quick and easy to use. So it's onto the bus and away as we look out of the window at the island once more on our way to our hotel. As the coach heads away from Skiathos Town airport and starts to drop off our fellow holiday makers who are staying closer to Skiathos Town. For us the sense of anticipation and excitement is steadily growing. After a few such stops the coach rounds the bend that leads down to Troulos village and trundles through the village and after rounding just one more bend there it is out of our left hand window the fabulous Troulos Bay Hotel. This is where we will spend the next two weeks enjoying all that this superb hotel has to offer. Every year the hotel owners make improvements to the external and internal facilities of the hotel. About 80% of their guests who stay at the hotel are repeat customers including Susie and I. So as our coach pulls into the hotel forecourt it is with much anticipation that we disembark, get our cases from the driver and make our way to the hotel reception to meet all our Greek friends once again…

Arriving at the Troulos Bay Hotel

Our friends George, Katia, Yannis and Yellis of the Troulos Bay Hotel
and the view from our balcony at the hotel

Up the Steps into the Troulos Bay Hotel: One year (2014) I injured my medial ligament in my right knee a few weeks before we went to Skiathos so when we arrived I needed a brief rest on the wall outside of reception. After a few minutes George the hotel manager came out to look for us and the smile of greeting he gave us made us feel welcome and right at home. We exchanged hugs and kiss then he took our cases inside for us before getting Dori to take them up to our room. Next out was head of security and reception Yannis who again gave us hugs and kisses before escorting us into the hotel to complete the formalities. The smiles on everyone's faces that we met whilst booking in made us realise that we had arrived at our paradise hotel at last. We always have the same room when we stay at the hotel. It is on the top floor (1st floor) number 318. The hotel management had left us a greeting bottle of our favourite wine and a bowl of freshly cut roses in the room. As well as this they had mounted one of my framed watercolour paintings on our room wall beside our bed that I had given them in 2010. No greater compliment could I have and this thoughtful touch is so typical of the hotel management. Susie and I always walk out onto our balcony as soon as we get in our room to wonder once more at the view of the pool, beach, the small island of Touranes and beyond that to the large island of Evia. Doing this is one of the many highlights that we have looked forward to all year…

Arriving at the Troulos Bay Hotel

Susie outside the Troulos Bay Hotel and us in the hotel restaurant

Having first unpack our things and then taken a walk up to the local shop (which has everything one would need for your holiday) to get water, milk (we have a fridge in the room) and kitchen rolls so we can make a drink whenever we want (we always take our own kettle) it was time to go downstairs for our first evening meal. Over the years we have made good friends with the staff of the hotel and always look forward to seeing Ervin (head waiter) and the family that runs the hotel so well (George, Yellis, Katherine, Yannis, Katia and Alexei). The first evening when we sit at our usual table at the front of the restaurant for our meal is always a very special moment. In the Troulos Bay Hotel restaurant, over the years,the menu has altered very little but has several nice dishes to consider and there is always fresh fish on the menu which suits me just fine. They also have a bottle of our favourite Cretan dry white wine in an ice bucket and two wine glasses waiting on our table when we get down for our first meal so we can toast our arrival in paradise. After we say hello and have a chat with the waiters Ervin, Tim, Michel and Vangelis we settle down to our first meal of our holiday. The meal was great and the wine went down very well...

Arriving at the Troulos Bay Hotel

Karl, Anna, Andy and Lynn at Troulos Bay

In recent years the hotel has installed a large swimming pool and pool bar in the gardens that face the beach and sea. When we have spent the day on our sun beds on the beach and swam in the warm blue sea, we often go back into the hotel grounds and have a swim in the pool and a few drinks at the pool bar in the late afternoon. Sometimes Andrew, Lynn, Alistair, Issy, Karl, Anna or Dori will join us for a drink. We will then go up to our room for coffee on the balcony (you should always make time for a coffee) before showering and going down for our evening meal or even out on the town. Susie and I are early risers so we often take a walk around the pretty gardens of the hotel before going onto the beach for a spot of beach combing before 7.30 am. The gardens, pool and beach are kept spotless by Dori who also finds the time to play beach tennis daily at 4 pm with our friend Andrew from Sheffield who along with his wife Lynn also stay at the hotel the same weeks we do. Over the years we have made good friends with some of our fellow guests so as well as Andrew and Lynn we often spend some time talking to Alistair and Issy from Scotland and Karl and Anna from Vienna in Austria who also stay at the hotel the same weeks we do…

Arriving at the Troulos Bay Hotel

Alan, Susie, Harry at the hotel and sunshades, a cat and palm trees

Although we venture out to other restaurants both in Troulos village and in Skiathos Town from time to time we have most of our evening meals in the hotel restaurant. In the mornings we often have some breakfast on our balcony. I usually have a cake and a cup of tea whilst Susie has just a cup of coffee (you should always find time for a coffee). It is a great way to start off the day. The days we spend on Troulos Bay beach we tend to have lunch in the hotel beach front restaurant or on rare occasions we have eaten in the hotel inside restaurant if the weather is unkind so the guest have three options/choices of hotel eating locations in which to have their meal…

Arriving at the Troulos Bay Hotel

Ervin and some of the hotel restaurant team

Susie and I go to the Mediterranean, like most people, because the weather and temperature is generally better than we get in the UK however, at mid-day the heat and the sun can get more than one can bear so Susie and I will often be found in the beach side restaurant not just to eat and drink but to find some welcome shade. The happy and smiling company of Ervin, the other hotel staff and our guest friends makes this such an enjoyable experience that sometimes we even forget to go back onto the beach! Above we see Susie waiting for her lunch to arrive but like many ladies she also comes prepared, which is great for me, with her beach bag that contains books, water, cameras and much, much more. So after we have eaten we can stay seated in the shade and have an hour or so relaxing with a good book or chatting to fellow guests while we enjoy perhaps a nice cup of coffee or a cold beer whilst relaxing for after all this is just what holidays are for. A significant amount of our holiday we spend sitting on our balcony enjoying the superb view and the sunny warm weather however, as those who travel to the Greek islands will know that when it rains in Greece it really rains very hard and again we are fortunate that our balcony has a roof extending over it so we can continue to sit and look out to sea even in thunderstorms. This not only means that we can continue to watch ships sail by but also we have been lucky enough to see dolphins swimming by. Another good thing about holidaying in Greece is that the rain clouds soon pass and the sun soon comes out once again. So even when it rains we still feel that we are in paradise…

Arriving at the Troulos Bay Hotel

Hotel managers Katie and Yannis with Alan and Susie in the hotel restaurant

One thing that we really like about our hotel is that the management are always smiling and happy to help in any way they can. Above we see Katie and Yannis members of the management team of the hotel having a well earned rest. I have already mentioned how Susie and I enjoy our swim in the hotel pool in the late afternoon but another thing we enjoy about our balcony overlooking the pool is being able to watch Dori working to keep the pool clean and tidy in the morning and again in the early evenings. I wonder how many people notice how hard he works to ensure our enjoyment is not spoilt when using this lovely facility. He always finds the time to wave and smile and sometimes he joins us for a drink at the pool bar before Susie and I go up to our room in the early evening. Some days when on holiday there is nothing better than having an ice cold beer at lunchtime and people watch or just sit back and enjoy the fantastic view. I notice that people sometimes do the most funny things and I often use some of the actions that I see or the views that I have enjoyed so much to do a watercolour painting when I get back home. I often bring back these paintings framed up the next year to give a s a gift to the hotel family and staff or one of our other Skiathan friends. At dusk the sky takes on many different colours and one of the memorable events of our holiday takes place every evening at 8.45 pm! While we sit at our front row table in the restaurant one of natures great spectacles takes to the evening sky. About 12 to 14 kites swoop down from the pine covered hills behind Troulos Bay and swoop over the sea enjoying themselves whilst giving us a great free show. After about 15 to 20 minutes they fly back to their hills for the night…

Arriving at the Troulos Bay Hotel

Susie and Alan at Troulos Bay on Skiathos

In recent years we have got into the habit of going down for our evening meal earlier so we can spend an hour or so chatting to the hotel manager George in the lounge bar. Not only does George manage the hotel all day but he spends his evenings running the bar as well. He works so very hard. We chat about his family and he asks us about our life back home in the UK. He also makes me my favourite drink called Cuba Libra which he makes with a whole squeezed lime, lots and lots of Bacardi and a little dash of coke. Our friends Alistair and Issy sometimes join us for a drink and a chat before Susie and I go into the restaurant for our wine and meal and to watch the kites flyby...

Exploring Skiathos Town

The local bus
that takes us into
Skiathos Town…

The Town of Skiathos

On the first full day of our holiday and on some other days of our holiday we walk up the lane leading from our hotel to catch the local bus into Skiathos Town at bus stop 20. We usually go into Town three or four times during the day and a couple of evenings during our stay on the island to enjoy all that Skiathos Town has to offer. Sometimes our friends Andrew and Lynn join us especially if we are going to Ervin's brother's restaurant called the Bakaliko (his name is Bello). It is right on the shores of Skiathos Town in the bay of the New Port where he is the head chef. On the next few pages we will get on the local bus and go into Town to see some of our holiday snaps and read about the experiences that Susie and I have had during our visits to the Town of Skiathos over the years…

Exploring Skiathos Town

Skiathos old port and the Bourtzi diving board

Skiathos Town, the islands "Capital"is the only large town on the island. It is built on two low hills, rising above the twin harbours of the New Port and the Old Port where you will see many smart sailing yachts, luxurious motor cruisers, excursion boats and fishing boats. The first three types of boats now outnumber the dwindling fishing fleet anchored at the far end of the old port. Between the new and old ports and connected to the harbour esplanade by a short causeway, is the tiny, pine covered islet called the Bourtzi. At the far end of which is a cafe that overlooks a diving board where the local children can often be seen enjoying themselves by taking turns diving into the warm blue sea. There loud screams of pleasure and joy can easily be heard all around the Bourtzi as they try to make as big a splash as they can by jumping or diving off the diving board…

Exploring Skiathos Town

Susie at the windmill cafe and a plane heading for the end of the runway

As I have already mentioned Susie and I always travel into Skiathos Town from our resort by the local bus service (Troulos Bay bus stop 20) at least four or five times during our two weeks holiday and disembark at the town bus station (bus stop 0). As we arrive at the station to our right is one of the town schools, to our left is a small memorial garden plaza. To the front of the bus and across the main road is the bus operators office. Looking behind us and to the left is the New Port promenade with all the yachts moored leading up to the ferry port and main town area whilst to the right is the road that leads along the bay passing several good restaurants including the Bakaliko where Bello works and a bit further down the road is the Windmill Cafe where Susie and I often sit and have a Frappe (iced coffee) and then as you go around a bend you will see the end of the airport runway…

Exploring Skiathos Town

Flying past the windmill cafe into Skiathos airport

A frappe by the sea at the Windmill cafe in the bay of Skiathos Town

Exploring Skiathos Town

The Wind taverna and a view of the old port in Skiathos Town

Alan and the Skiathos Town statue

Exploring Skiathos Town

A narrow street in Skiathos Town and hanging the fish out to dry

The town's narrow streets (see above) of Skiathos Town are lined with whitewashed houses, typically with bright-painted wrought-iron balconies, red-tiled roofs, wooden shutters and small courtyards that are made more colourful by pots of geraniums, basil and purple or scarlet bougainvillea. The town is well endowed with pubs, bars and cafes beside its two harbours that are originally called the old and new harbours. The ferry port nestles between where these tow harbours meet. There are plenty of good restaurants overlooking the waterfront and also up many of the narrow side streets that run up hill away from the waterfront. Day trip boats and water -taxis leave every morning from the old port for the busy beaches along the south coast and others venture around the islands less crowded north, west and east coast beaches…

Exploring Skiathos Town

The statue in the old port Skiathos Town

The narrow streets of Skiathos Town

Exploring Skiathos Town

High and dry in Skiathos Bay

Skiathos Town cat and a fishing boat in the old port

Exploring Skiathos Town

Cat in a taverna, George and Eve of the Mythos Cafe

When we are in Skiathos Town Susie and I always find time for a coffee and on a very warm day there is nothing better than having an ice cold frappe while sitting at a table at the Windmill Cafe looking at the boats in the bay and watching the planes swooping in to land with there landing wheels just above the surface of the sea. Over the many years that we have been visiting the island of Skiathos we have always found that with it's great olives, fabulous Greek salad, tasty fresh fish and a refreshing cold drink (wine-beer-frappe) all you then need is good company. We find this by spending time with the staff at our hotel and our friends in Skiathos Town both at the windmill cafe and at the Mythos cafe. We find their company always provides us with very good company, friendly chatter and much, much more…

Exploring Skiathos Town

Susie and Alan enjoying a cold beer in Skiathos Town

Exploring Skiathos Town

Susie at the Windmill Cafe and the airport runway in Skiathos Bay

Skiathos Town has three pretty churches rising above the red-tiled roofs of it's 18th century houses. Compared with many Greek settlements, it's quite a modern town. For many centuries, the islanders lived in the fortified village of Kastro, high above the sea on the northern tip of Skiathos. After Susie and I have finished our frappe at the windmill we often walk along the new port promenade passing the ferry port on our left and the main shopping street on our right before walking passed the causeway to the Bourtzi and onto the old port. After this fairly long walk in the sun it is time for a few cold beers with George and Eve at the Mythos Cafe…

Exploring Skiathos Town

Susie and Alan in the Selini restaurant and the lone violinist on the Bourtzi

In the 1830's, when the Sporades, along with most of Greece, gained independence the people of the island built Skiathos Town and the Bourtzi was then built as a fortress. The Bourtzi is now home to the islands theatre and a pleasant open air cafe under the pine trees, with great views across the vividly blue water. There is also a diving board at the end of the Bourtzi where the local children can be seen most days practicing their diving skills or just having fun. We have enjoyed watching the children play and also listening to the local lone violinist that sometimes plays in the shade of the pines on a bench on the Bourtzi...

Exploring Skiathos Town

The old port in Skiathos Town

Exploring Skiathos Town

The statue, walking in the old port and plane about to land on Skiathos

Because of my poorly knees walking around Skiathos Town can be quite challenging as much of the town is reached up steep narrow alley's which can be treacherous when wet. Even when it is dry you still will need your wits about you as not only people, cycles and motor bikes but also cars and vans come at you from all directions in the narrow streets. The main shopping street runs up the hill away from the ferry port entrance and has shops left and right nearly to the top where you will find one of the towns schools, a pharmacy and several good restaurants...

Exploring Skiathos Town

The statue, the windmill cafe and a local fisherman mending his nets

Exploring Skiathos Town

Susie at the windmill cafe and Alan at the Mythos cafe

When in Skiathos Town, if you walk down past the gates into the ferry port and around the bend at the Bourtzi the promenade will lead you to one of Susie and my favourite parts of Skiathos Town the old port. There is nothing better than to sit in the Mythos Cafe and people watch as tourists and locals constantly walk past all day. Often after many drinks and maybe, it has got dark it is just as good sitting there watching the locals in their best cloths come and stroll up and down the well illuminated promenade exchanging greetings with other local Greek residence, friends and tourists alike. They also have their well behaved children with them who also look very smart…

Exploring Skiathos Town

It's frappe time

Every year that we have holidayed on the Island of Skiathos at the Troulos Bay Hotel we have arrived on the island on a Friday afternoon and gone into Skiathos Town on our first full day on the Saturday. We do this because it gives us a chance to get use to the strength and heat of the sun for the first full day. It also helps that we can walk around and be protected by the shaded narrow alleys and the bar canopies like those at the Windmill Cafe and the Mythos Cafe. Saturdays is also the day when many peoples holidays either begin or end on the island so the Town is always very quite as a result. This gives us more space to walk around in and enjoy our first full day on our paradise Island in relative peace. The best thing of all is that you can call into any taverna or cafe you like in Town and enjoy an ice cold frappe...

Exploring Skiathos Town

Coming into land, the old port and the Skiathos Town statue

It is very sad that the Island of Skiathos suffered greatly from bombings and other atrocities during the second world war. Many islanders were killed during the conflict and so as soon as they could after the war they erected the statue that is on the waterfront on the corner of the bourtzi and the old port. This was not only to commemorate those that were lost but also to celebrate their rich fishing heritage and to honour all those who had suffered or died during all of the other conflicts that have occurred on the island in the past…

Exploring Skiathos Town

The picture taker and the 2014 holiday winning snap taken by YES it was Susie!

Susie and I, on every holiday, take part in and enjoy our own annual holiday photographic competition to see which of us can capture the best snap of our holiday! Here we see Susie sitting on a bench on the Bourtzi getting ready to take a picture of me taking a picture of her snapping me! Just one of the silly things that we do on holiday but of course I think that I always manage to take the best snap but I am sure Susie would not agree and tell you that she does. Actually to be honest she usually wins!…

Exploring Skiathos Town

The streets of Skiathos Town

The main shopping street in Skiathos Town is really for accuracy just about the only tourist shopping street in town. I have already mentioned that the town streets are very narrow and steep but as you can see from the picture above I was not exaggerating so be careful when out shopping or just out for a walk in town. Sometimes when you are walking down any of the narrow streets of town you will see the local people going about their daily lives and wonder just how they manage to coup in the winter as we know that sometimes they do get snow and the surfaces of the streets must be very treacherous when this happens. Our Skiathan friends have told us this and even had photographs to prove it! Also as you walk around the alley's and street's of Skiathos Town you should always keep your wits about you because of the already warned about traffic that can appear out of nowhere right in front or behind you but please when it is safe to do so look up! Many, if not all, of the houses in the town have balconies some of which are relatively unadorned but many do have cascading pots of flowers of every type and colour. Some locals also leave their house windows or doors open and you can often hear Greek music being played from within…

Exploring Skiathos Town

The house of Papadiamantis and the main shopping street in Skiathos Town

The house of Papadiamantis is well worth a visit during your stay on the island. This pretty little museum is tucked away on a small square just off the main shopping street about 100 meters up on the right from the port end of the street. It celebrates the life of the island's most famous son. He was a journalist, philosopher and author. His full name was Alexandros Papadiamantis (1851-1911). The islands international airport is named after him. I am lucky enough to have one of his books of short stories and I have enjoyed reading his accounts of the customs of the people of Skiathos from days gone by very much. The main shopping street is also named after this famous son of Skiathos. The museum is housed in the house where he actually lived, worked and died and contains some of his furniture and is adorned with photographs, manuscripts and portraits of the author and his works and is well worth a visit…

Exploring Skiathos Town

The streets and cats of Skiathos Town

Sometimes you can walk around the back streets of Skiathos Town and not see another soul but you also know that at any moment a motor cycle, van or car may come charging around the corner so it pays to listen for the tell tale noise such vehicles have. In the case of motor cycles just think of Freddy the Frog and get ready to hop out of the way! There is however, one big advantage of walking in the narrow streets of Skiathos Town and that is that you can often be totally in the shade on one side of the street and in full sun just a side step away! Susie and I, when in town, often wander around the streets of the town to admire the bougainvillea flower's cascading down from the balconies and also to see the numerous cats that seem to sit on every town house wall, steps or lay in the sun beside the house entrances. As you wonder around the town make sure you greet those that you meet on the way as the people of Skiathos, like all Greeks, are very friendly and approachable. It is worth remembering that they live at a much slower pace than we do in the UK and as mentioned several times before, unlike many of us in the UK, they always find the time for a chat and/or a coffee!…

Exploring Skiathos Town

Skiathos Town views, Susie and Alan raising their glass of cold beer to those intrepid climbers (mentioned below) whilst we are resting in the Mythos Cafe

The church at the top of the hill that overlooks the ferry port and much of the town of Skiathos is a favourite place for tourist to visit. Susie and I can be sitting in the Mythos Cafe having a drink when a ferry or day trip boat calls into port and watch with admiration as the visitors, led by someone with a raised umbrella, Scurry off up the very steep steps to get to the platform in front of the church high above for the fantastic views that this vantage point offers. Many make the arduous journey to the top to see where the opening letter posting sequence was filmed for the blockbuster film Mamma Mia. We often watch the DVD of the film before we come on our holiday to Skiathos to help set the scene. Meanwhile, high above us and mission accomplished the visitors scurry back down the steps to once more board their boat and set sail for places unknown while Susie and I sit back and continue to enjoy our cold drinks in our cool and un-flustered haven of the Mythos Cafe…

Exploring Skiathos Town

Skiathos Town church on the hill and Troulos Bay beach

Finding ourselves rather worn out by watching all of the busy activity in Skiathos Town. So after yet another boat comes into port and disgorges another horde of sightseeing tourists that also venture up the steep steps to the top of the hill to visit the church we decide to head back home. Or rather back to our wonderful hotel that by now feels just like home! Susie and I make our way slowly back along the waterfront back to the bus station to catch the local bus back to the Troulos Bay Hotel. It is not unusual that as we walk back to catch the bus we come to the unanimous decision that tomorrow we will spend the day relaxing, swimming and sunbathing on the Troulos Bay beach and so that is where we will be going in the next chapter...

Relaxing at Troulos Bay

The beach at Troulos Bay

As the name suggests Troulos Bay beach is a curving bay of fine soft golden sand. Susie and I have been going to the Troulos Bay Hotel for many years. The main reason that we choose this hotel, in the first place, was its fantastic facilities and having the sandy beach that is only a small step from the hotels garden. On the beach the access to the warm blue sea is gently sloping and is sandy underfoot which helps everyone safely access and egress the sea. The hotel also has the concession to hire the sun beds and parasols immediately in front of the hotel. The hotel management have thankfully, decided to position the pairs of sunbeds and parasol, they own, with extra space between them and the next pair which is great for us users. Unfortunately this extra space is not always the case on other beaches on the island…

Relaxing at Troulos Bay

Early morning on Troulos Bay beach, sunbeds and Susie on the beach

Susie and I are early risers even when we are on holiday. We will often go for an early morning walk on Troulos Bay beach. Whilst we are on the beach and if we are planning to spend the day in the resort we will select what sunbeds we will use for sunbathing that day. Once selected we will put our beach towels on them. We usually select a pair of sunbeds that are on the front row because these are the nearest to the sea thus reducing the distance that I have to hobble to get into the sea. Another big advantage of Troulos Bay beach is that the sand gently shelves into the water making it easier for me to get in and out of the sea...

Relaxing at Troulos Bay

Our balcony view…

View from our balcony and the boat behind the shade on Troulos Bay beach

On our holidays to Troulos Bay we not only see the beach deserted in the early morning but we also see the beach emptying as the sun sets on yet another beautiful day. We get these views from either our hotel room balcony that overlooks the beach or from the front row seats in the hotel restaurant. As you know Susie and I try to outdo each others photography skills by trying to get the best holiday snap on all our holidays. The above picture of the boat behind the shade was a real beauty and very atmospheric. I was taken by Susie in 2013 and was judged by us both as being the best picture of the 2013 holiday season!…

Relaxing at Troulos Bay

Our abandoned sunbeds at lunchtime and a view of the Troulos Bay beach

On the days that we spend on the beach at Troulos Bay you can often see our selected sunbeds left deserted over the lunchtime period. Although we do plan to return, rest and perhaps have another swim in the afternoon we often abandon our sunbeds to get away from the heat of the midday sun as it beats down from high overhead. This, for us, is when staying at the Troulos Bay Hotel really pays off because we can either choose to go up to our balcony for tea/coffee and a light snack or use the hotel beach side restaurant for a lunch of perhaps olives, a Greek salad and/or a pizza or even egg, bacon and chips which is my personal favourite accompanied by cold beer or wine. Most days, that we spend at our resort, we tend to do the later so we can chat to other guests and/or to the very friendly hotel staff…

Relaxing at Troulos Bay

Boats, floats and the island off Troulos Bay beach

On the days when we decide to have our lunch in the hotel beach side restaurant we often choose a table that overlooks the beach. We usually spend 2 or 3 hours over having lunch, a few drinks and maybe even reading for awhile. When sitting in the restaurant we are always amazed at seeing the heat haze rising off the sand, sea and reflecting off the sunshade parasols. The holidaymakers, unlike us, that have remained on the beach over the lunchtime period are having to constantly move their sunbeds to keep in the limited shade of their sunshades. Their determination and endurance to stay on the beach at all costs says much about the attitude of the people of the holidaymaker! Thankfully we do not share their desire and are therefore, not one of their number! All this means however, that a sunshade is an absolute must have essential for the many intrepid holiday makers who steadfastly remain on the beach during the mid-day period or failing this for many maybe, regular trips into the sea to cool off may offer a solution to this potential burning situation!…

Relaxing at Troulos Bay

Shades on Troulos Bay beach, the Troulos Bay Hotel and the Hotel cats

On our holidays to the Troulos Bay Hotel we have noticed, over the years, that the hotel management had not only made numerous improvements to the exterior and interior of the hotel but had also made improvements to the beach based facilities and equipment since we had visited them the year previously. New room, facilities, décor, fixtures, fittings and a new pool have all been introduced over the years. The beach sunbeds and parasols have been changed several times over the years however, the current greater comfort design of the sunbeds and larger parasols have been there for the last few years. We have over the years however, seen several different designs of parasols used over the years including a shaggy style that was preferred some years ago but these only lasted just one season. I expect that they did not respond to well to being buffeted by the occasionally strong winds and torrential rain that the resort can sometimes experience! The latest bamboo covered parasols shown above and on the previous page have now lasted several years but I would not be surprised if these have been replaced when we next go to the Troulos Bay Hotel!…

Relaxing at Troulos Bay

Andy, Alan, some of the friendly hotel staff , Susie, Lynn, Yannis and Alan all enjoying a relaxing lunchtime together at the hotel

Some days on the Troulos Bay beach it gets so hot at lunchtime that even the most dedicated sun worshiper relents and leaving the beach to the sun and discarding the comfort of their sun beds they adjourn to the comfort and shade of the Troulos Bay Hotel pool bar, restaurant and/or their balcony for a few hours of respite. When this happens it is great to sit with friends in the shade, over a nice cold beer and compare notes on where everyone has been on the island so far. It is also the time when you find out what restaurants they have tried, where these are and if they would recommend them to other!...

Relaxing at Troulos Bay

The tennis match with Andy resting afterwards with Lynn

Every day of our holiday to the Troulos Bay Hotel a special event takes place on the sandy Troulos Bay beach. At 4 pm it is time for the local tennis tournament between our friends Andy and Dori. Dori is the hotel handyman, beach and pool attendant. These matches last about an hour or until someone collapses and are not for the faint hearted. This is because Dori belts the ball as hard as he can at Andrew who often returns them with interest much to Dori's dismay. It is important to know that Dori can often be less that accurate with his serves or returns so those of us resting on our sunbeds need to be on constant alert for low flying tennis balls whilst watching the game or not!. So those not watching the match beware!…

Relaxing at Troulos Bay

The Sea gently lapping onto Troulos Bay beach with yachts sailing by

On Troulos Bay beach after the big match the beach settles back down and the children and adults can safely resume their sand castle building or just sitting on the sea edge and letting the waves cascade over them. Although Troulos Bay has little tidal action at set times of the day it does have times when the sea suddenly starts putting quite big waves onto the shoreline. At first this can be disconcerting to the visitor but soon you will realise that it is only the bow waves of a large ferry or tanker passing beyond the little island of Touranes just offshore which is sending the waves it creates into the bay to break on the seashore. So do not be concerned it will not harm you and so all is still well with the world, however, sometimes, very really, the waves and/or tremors could be caused by the occasional earthquake. After all you are holidaying in an active plate tectonic area! We have only experienced one seismic event in all the years that we have been visiting the island and we are still alive to tell the tale!...

Relaxing at Troulos Bay

Alan on our hotel balcony and early morning on Troulos Bay Beach

As you already know Susie and I go early morning walking (beachcomber) on Troulos Bay beach every morning of our holiday but one thing I forgot to mention was that we always try and take some pieces of bread with us! Why you may ask do we take bread with us on our walk? Well the answer to that question can be found on page 74 but in the meantime (wait for it) I think the picture of the deserted sunbeds above gives a sense of the peace and quite the early riser can enjoy when they are out and about on Troulos Bay beach. As a footnote: Obviously both Susie and I often eat some of the bread ourselves as you can see from the picture of me doing just that above taken one early morning before we set off on our daily beach combing expedition of the day! So why do we take some bread with us? Answer later!…

Relaxing at Troulos Bay

Alan all at sea, the beach and Susie floating in the sea off Troulos Bay

When at Troulos Bay you can not help but notice how much bluer the sea and the sky seems to be when you are on a Greek Island in the Mediterranean Sea. The sun also ensures that the sea is not only azure and warm but is oh so inviting as well. Us UK based visitors find it amazing to not only be able to beach comb and paddle comfortably in the sea at any time but also to be able to go in for a cooling swim either in the early morning, during the day and/or even late in the evening whilst still retain all your precious parts intact and not to have them frozen off like you would if you swam in the north sea!…

Relaxing at Troulos Bay

Early evening calm and my mermaid (Susie)in the sea at Troulos Bay

In 2006 I managed to win our yearly photography holiday competition, for the first time, with the above picture of the rare Troulos Bay "Mermaid" just sitting on a rock just off the beach. I was so please to get this recognition that it inspired me to try and win the competition every year thereafter, unfortunately this ambition has eluded me every year since as Susie has enjoyed reminding me of all to often. As you will all probably know the picture is actually of Susie and is not really a mermaid. I mention this just incase this is not obvious to everyone…

Relaxing at Troulos Bay

A yacht sailing past and Susie looking out to sea at Troulos Bay

On Troulos Bay beach, when you are very hot, it is often a relief to be able to stand on the seashore and let the waves cool your feet which in turn makes you feel much cooler. By holidaying on an island, such as Skiathos, you often find that you will get cooling breezes off the sea throughout the day but beware they also speed up the skin burning process so wear the appropriate sunscreen. These breezes also help to keep you cool but sometimes it is just being able to stand with your toes in the warm sea and watch the ships sail by with the sun on your back is all the relaxation you need. I think Susie is enjoying all of the above. Remember you are on holiday so enjoy every minute of every day!...

Relaxing at Troulos Bay

Heads up and when the boats comes in at Troulos Bay

Are you ready with your bread in hand for it is the time to go for a walk on Troulos Bay beach in the early morning! The reason Susie and I try to take some pieces of bread with us when we go for our usual early morning walk along the beach is because there are Terrapins and fish in a small fresh water river that comes down from the surrounding hills and flows right up to the back of the beach at Troulos Bay. To find this little treasure you need to turn right along the beach from the hotel or from the lane that runs down to the beach from the shop on the main road and walk along the beach for about 200 meters. Keep an eye out on your right for the telltale sign of the little river which is off to your right. Susie and I, along with many other holidaymakers, love going along to the river to feed these little fellows…

Relaxing at Troulos Bay

Troulos Bay beach and fishing boats in the old port in Skiathos Town

As the waves lap onto Troulos Bay beach Susie and I have decided that we will leave this idyllic spot and walk up the lane to bus stop 20 and get the local bus into town once more to spend some quality time in Skiathos Town. Something Susie and I do on several daytimes but also on a couple of evenings as well during our stay on the island. On these occasions we always find the time to spend some of our time in the old port area of town and that is where we are heading in the next chapter…

Enjoying the Old Port in Skiathos Town

The water taxi, the fish market and a painting of Skiathos Town

There is more than just one way to get to Skiathos Town from Troulos Bay. One is much more straight forward than the others. For example you could just catch the bus and go straight into town. If you want to take the more difficult route you could make your way either by walking or on the local bus to Koukounaries bus stop 28. Once there you can then catch the water taxi moored in the small harbour and go from Koukounaries to old port in town. You could even make your way to one of the other south coast resorts that also has the water taxi operating from there waterfront and make your way to the old port in Skiathos Town that way. The water taxi offers you a completely different perspective of the island than if you use only the bus. For example, you will see the coast cascading down to the sea on the taxi plus as you enter the old port and travel passed the Bourtzi to your right you will get a view of the town that is truly amazing. In the harbour of the old port you will see the cruise boats all lined up that do the around the island cruises and other excursions. Behind them are the bars and cafes and the jetty where your water taxi will drop you off and pick you up again. In the old port you can also see what is left of the local fishing fleet with the fish market near the far end of the Port. However, you get there, once there, you will find the effort is reward tenfold as there is real beauty and interest in the old port and the surrounding area!…

Enjoying the Old Port in Skiathos Town

Alan, the Mythos Cafe and Susie on the old port promenade

In the old port in Skiathos Town is the canopied bar of the Mythos Cafe. We have been using this cafe on every occasion that we have gone into town over the years. Over this time we have made friends with the owners George and Eve and we have enjoyed their hospitality often. Susie and I have spent many a happy hour enjoying several cold drinks, snakes and sometime we have had a very good lunchtime meal in the cafe. One of our favourite meals is a BLT or you may know it as a bacon, lettuce and tomato sandwich accompanied by or course chips! This is often while we are sitting relaxing and just watching the world go by from the comfort of our vantage point at an outdoor table and chairs. Of course always with an ice cold frappe and/or a few cold beers. After a period of time, having enjoyed the company, food and drink we often take a wander along the quay and/or up the nearby shopping street. The old port and the surrounding area is often quieter than you would think at certain times of the day and especially during the early afternoon hours when everyone seems to be sensibly resting. This is also a good time for holidaymakers to visit and explore all that the old port area has to offer…

Enjoying the Old Port in Skiathos Town

Mending the nets in the old port and a cat relaxing in the mended nets

One day whilst Susie and I were on holiday on the Island of Skiathos we were taking a stroll along the old port harbour promenade in the section that most of the local fishing boats are located when we noticed some of the local fishermen busy mending their nets on the quay side. It is something you see quite often on many of the Greek islands. To add more interest to this scene of men at work we had to smile at the enterprising cat that had found the ideal bed to relax on. The cat was laying on the pile of nets that the fishermen had already mended and they had left in a neat pile unattended. The cat looked as snug as a bug in a rug!...

Enjoying the Old Port in Skiathos Town

Fishing in the moon light and returning back to port

The Skiathos Town fishermen shown mending their nets in the old port on the previous page were so engrossed in their work that they did not seem to notice the many tourists that were taking photographs of them. Meanwhile the cat relaxing on the pile of mended nets just could not have cared less as long as she/he had a comfortable bed. We have seen the local fishermen take their boats out of the old port in the evening to fish out to sea. Once there they use a floodlight that is fitted to the prow of their boat which they shine down into the water to attract the fish. After a full nights fishing and if they have been lucky and caught some fish they return to the old port and sell what they do not personally need. This they do at the small fish market building which is immediately behind the tables that are shown where the net menders are working on the previous page…

Enjoying the Old Port in Skiathos Town

Boats viewed from the sloop from the old port, George of the Mythos cafe and Alan enjoying a meal at the Lo and La restaurant in the old port

One thing to look out for when you are strolling around the old port is the amazing glimpses that you get of the fishing boats anchored in the old port. This happens when you make your way up the slope that leads up from the far end of the old port quay . When you reach the top of the slope and turn left you will pass several good quality restaurants. Susie and I have often made our way up the sloop to have our lunch and/or evening meal at one of these eating establishments which overlook the old port. The restaurants including the Selini (the wind), Lo and La and Stematis. All are very good and we have never been disappointed with our meals. The well appointed eating establishment at the top of the sloop provide fantastic meals plus maybe better than that is the fantastic views of the old port, fishing boats and the Bourtzi that the tables at the front of these restaurants gives you…

Enjoying the Old Port in Skiathos Town

Alan above the old port, a town restaurant and a view of the old port

Susie and I, when on holiday and visiting Skiathos Town, have often made the climb up the steep steps leading away from the old port to have a light meal and a few glasses of cold frappe, beer and or wine up at one of the restaurant situated high up and looking down on the old port waterfront . Having been refreshed we also, on our way back down the steps, often stop and enjoy the superb views that this vantage point offers…

Enjoying the Old Port in Skiathos Town

The Mythos Cafe and the view of the old port promenade from the cafe

It may be sad to say this but it is true that every time Susie and I go into Skiathos Town be it during the day time or in the evening we **ALWAYS** stop for a while (often a long while) at the Mythos Cafe to meet once more our friends George and Eve who run the cafe bar in the old port. I have already mentioned that we always make a point on the first day of our holiday to go into Skiathos Town when we always call into the Mythos Cafe. We do this so we can exchange gifts with George and Eve and find out how each others year has gone since we last saw each other. We have been doing this for as many years as we have been going to the island and George and Eve are always very pleased to see us once again and welcome us often with a complementary drink…

Enjoying the Old Port in Skiathos Town

Boats in Skiathos bay, Alan and Susie in the Mythos Cafe in the old port

When Susie and I have made our way to the old port and made ourselves comfortable in the Mythos cafe were we often just sit and relax and cool down for a long time especially if we have previously been shopping or even just walking around in the sun. Obviously we are however, ready for an ice cold drink! Our friend George, who runs the Mythos cafe ,who is in the orange tee shirt over my right shoulder in the picture above, will soon notice our arrival. In only a matter of a few seconds he will come over and ask us what we would like. He will also have a big smile of greeting on his face. Sometimes, we find that this is the hardest decision of the day in deciding what we will have to drink!…

Enjoying the Old Port in Skiathos Town

Boats bobbing up and down in the old port harbour

When you are in the Mythos Cafe it is not unusual to see a group or two of local Greeks drinking small cups of coffee (you should always find time for a coffee) and playing a game of backgammon. In recent years this everyday activity has somewhat been replaced and now many Greeks are sitting alone using their laptops and/or other electronic hand held devices/equipment (much like most people do in the UK). In my opinion this is a real shame as the backgammon games would have always generated much discussion and laughter from those playing and created an active and enjoyable atmosphere. I believe that sometimes progress and change of this kind is not always the best thing for a society!...

Enjoying the Old Port in Skiathos Town

George, Alan and local cats in the Mythos Cafe

We are confident that you are always sure of a warm welcome from George and Eve at the Mythos Cafe Bar in the old port should you visit this cafe when you are in Skiathos Town. Most Greeks are very welcoming, friendly and happy to display their happiness at seeing/meeting any visitor by hugging and kissing them. So when you meet a Greek man or woman for that matter be prepared for hugs and kisses. This may not always be welcome, at first, by many of the UK male visitors because they may see these actions as to intrusive and unwanted but please remember that this behaviour is part of their culture where showing open affection is the norm! So please drop that English stiff upper lip attitude and get hugging back!...

Enjoying the Old Port in Skiathos Town

Eve and her daughter working in the Mythos Cafe

One day when Susie and I were sitting in the Mythos Cafe in the old port in Skiathos Town Susie took the above pictures. This was in 2013 and there are of Eve supervising her young daughter who was making herself useful by watering (saturating) the pots of flowers that are displayed all around the cafe. In Greece children are much loved and parents take great pride in seeing their offspring getting involved in the family business. Often in the years to come, and when the child has grown up. they will take over the business from their elders. It is often true that many Greek businesses involve not just mum, dad and their children but the grandparents as well! By having the whole extended family involved makes for a society that is based on the wider family and everyone working together…

Enjoying the Old Port in Skiathos Town

Lighting the Olympic torch and the torch coming past the Mythos Cafe

One day when we were on holiday on Skiathos in 2010 and we were sitting in the Mythos Cafe in the early evening enjoying a large cold beer each while we waited to see the Olympic runners and torch pass by the cafe. Everyone in the town was feeling very excited and you could sense their anticipation of waiting for this once in a lifetime experience! Today after all was a significant day for the people of Skiathos because Greece had staged the Olympics in 2008 and then in 2010 they held the special Para-Olympic games and to celebrate these events the Greek government had decided to share this achievement with all of the people of Greece. To do this the athletes and the Olympic torch was taken to everywhere throughout the Greek mainland and its inhabited islands. This was so that the Greek people could share in the nations pride and enjoyment (just like we did in the UK for the 2012 London Olympics). Today the people would see the torch being paraded around Skiathos Town. Luckily for us this included the athletes and torch coming right past where we were sitting in the old port. Like everyone else we waited with great excitement for them to pass us by so we could all stand up, clap and cheer them for their marvellous achievement. It was fantastic and will live long in our memory!…

Enjoying the Old Port in Skiathos Town

Raising our glasses in the Mythos Cafe
and the view from our hotel balcony

In 2014, whilst on holiday on Skiathos we once again took the bus to Skiathos Town and amongst other things we always spent some of our time in the Mythos cafe in the old port. Now just incase you thought that Susie did not also enjoy people watching from our seat within the Mythos Cafe as much as me you can see from the above picture that she also enjoyed the ambience and relaxation available while sitting in the cafe. One day during this holiday my luck was really in when Susie decided to leave me in the Mythos Cafe while she made her way into town and had a shopping trip up the towns main street. When she had left me to enjoy myself in the Mythos cafe I was a bit careful not to have too much to drink as it is quite a long walk back along the new port to the bus station at the far end to catch the bus to go back to the Troulos Bay Hotel. Meanwhile, while Susie was away, I took the photographs of the old port that are featured on the next page…

Enjoying the Old Port in Skiathos Town

Views of the old port in Skiathos Town

Enjoying the Old Port in Skiathos Town

Susie, Alan, the statue and a fishing boat all in the old port

When in Skiathos Town on a really hot day you can often find a slight breeze and some welcome shade by moving away from the harbour front and climbing the steps that lead up to the church that is just above the old port. Then if you then turn left up even more steps, around a corner until you reach the Selini taverna which is located on the left half way up the hill. We have often visited this taverna when we are on holiday. This is where you can sit on the front of the veranda that overlooks the old port, bourtzi and the ferry port and enjoy the cooling breeze as well as having an ice cold frappe, wine and/or beer and all with great views…

Enjoying the Old Port in Skiathos Town

A fishing boat and the day trip boats in the old port

Like everywhere in Greece, Skiathos Island, over the years, has seen the size of their fishing fleet reduce greatly. This obviously means that now fewer local men are involved in the fishing industry. The main reason for this probably rests with the EU, who a few years ago, in an attempt to preserve the diminishing stock of fish around Greece, offered fishermen cash settlements (Euros) to put their boats beyond use. As you can imagine many Greek fishermen took advantage of this windfall by pulling their boats up onto a beach somewhere and burning their beloved boat. When in the old port one fisherman told us that all you had to do was fill in a form (obviously), agree a date for the sad act and then an official would come and witness that you had actually destroyed your fishing boat (typical big brother or what)! This is a fact but it is all very sad but true!…

Enjoying the Old Port in Skiathos Town

The windmill restaurant on top of the hill in town and the Bourtzi

Often when Susie and I have visited Skiathos Town not only do we go into the old port, the town itself but also we like to wander around the Bourtzi. It is an amazing location just off the corner of the ferry port and the old port. Susie and I usually go onto the Bourtzi and have a coffee (you should always find time for a coffee) at the cafe at the far end of the Bourtzi. Whilst there we always spend a few minutes looking over the railings which overlooks the diving board and watch the local children enjoying themselves leaping off it and making as big a splash as they can. One day we even decided to leave the comforts of this cafe and make the steep climb up what seamed to me thousands of steps right up to the top of the town to visit the whitewashed Windmill restaurant. Going up and down all those steps was very hard and painful for my poorly knees and it is something that we have not done again!…

Enjoying the Old Port in Skiathos Town

The memorial statue, Skiathos bay, Susie and the old port

When you are on holiday on the Island of Skiathos you will see countless numbers of holidaymakers, when they visit the old port in Skiathos Town, strolling along the harbour front. There must be more pictures in peoples Skiathos holiday snaps collection of this scene than of any other. We are no different from the other visitors and as well as taking copious numbers of pictures we also like to see how many fishing boats have survived from last year, what has changed and what eating establishments have opened or closed along the promenade since our last stay on the Island…

Enjoying the Old Port in Skiathos Town

The old port in Skiathos Town

The old port waterfront promenade in Skiathos Town is often almost deserted if you know when to go. We have found that if you go on a Saturday morning it is very likely to be very quite. This is because many visitors are either arriving for their holiday or leaving the island to return back home. The old port is also often deserted at around 1 pm on most days because this is the hottest part of the day and most local people are having a siesta. Remember there is a perfectly good reason for having a siesta and staying out of the heat as any sensible person would not be walking around in the hot sunshine but be in the shade with a large ice cold frappe, a glass of wine and/or very large pint of beer. Just like we do when we are in town!…

Enjoying the Old Port in Skiathos Town

The waterfront and our friend George of the Mythos Cafe

When Susie and I have had a walk around Skiathos Town or even just around the old port it is always time for a rest, something to eat and a drink. For us this means that we will naturally find our way to the Mythos Cafe on the waterfront for a cold drink and maybe something to eat. Another nice thing about frequenting most Greek eating/drinking establishments is that they often give you complimentary dishes of snacks like crisps and/or nuts or even better still some local olives and/or pieces of fresh fruit. George and Eve have always done this for their customers and we think that this is a nice thing to do!…

Enjoying the Old Port in Skiathos Town

Runners and the people celebrating the Olympic parade in the old port

Whilst it is true that we have previously seen a picture of the Olympic runners in the old port in Skiathos Town. It was the time that Susie and I waited for them to come jogging past so we could toast them way back in 2010. I have repeated the picture that captures that moment when these brave individuals came jogging passed the Mythos Cafe in the Old Port as a tribute to them. The leader was holding the Olympic torch aloft for all to see and everyone including us applauded them and wished them well and thank them for their efforts in their quest for glory. The picture below this one shows the crowd of well wishers waiting for the runners to arrive back at the Bourtzi…

Enjoying the Old Port in Skiathos Town

Enjoying an early evening meal in the old port and the waterfront

We think that one of the best views in the Town of Skiathos is the old port and the Ferry port when seen from the steps which takes you passed Lo and La's restaurant and up towards the Selini. Although I have already mentioned this before I forgot to say that it is a very good idea when out sightseeing to wear a hat and sunglasses not just when you are out and about in Town but elsewhere on the island for that matter. Prevention is much better than getting burnt!…

Enjoying the Old Port in Skiathos Town

Susie and Alan enjoying a cold drink and a view of the town

Although it is true to say that one of the best locations on the island of Skiathos is the old port and the surrounding area of the town it should be remembered that there is more to this island than just Skiathos Town. As lovely as the town undoubtedly is there is much more to see and enjoy on the Island of Skiathos. Over the years that we have visited the island we have not only enjoyed our resort and the town but have loved experiencing the sights and sounds of the island. We have visited many of its sandy beaches, lovely villages, fantastic wildlife and enjoyed the magnificent scenery of the island. Also you can use any number of the local ferries and/or excursion boats that will take the holidaymaker to many of the nearby islands . These places are all well worth a visit during your holiday. In the next chapter we will go out and about around the Island of Skiathos and beyond…

Out and About

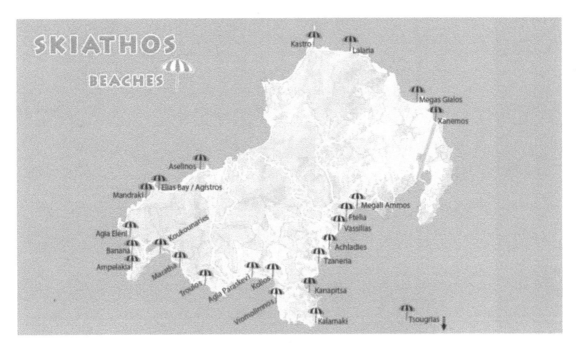

I know that we have previously been around the island of Skiathos in this book, however, this chapter, not only revisits some of those locations but adds some of our holiday tips and observations. Starting at the start of your holiday let us venture out and about together: First we would recommend that when you land at Skiathos airport that you keep an eye out for the free island maps that are available in the arrivals hall. It is a good idea to do this whilst waiting for your luggage to come around the carousel! Now that you have your map and luggage to hand it is time to make your way outside and start your holiday in the sun. Like most holiday makers we want to spend a large part of our time on holiday relaxing and enjoying the sun, sea and sand but you would be unwise not to take some time out to explore this truly beautiful island and beyond…

Out and About

The Troulos Bay bus stop, the local bus and Skiathos olives

During our holidays to the Island of Skiathos Susie and I have always spent at least four days and several evenings away from the Troulos Bay Hotel and the Troulos Bay beach to venture further afield and enjoy Skiathos Town and/or some of the sandy beaches that await you around the island. We have mainly used the superb local bus service for our transport needs. This is because it is reliable, reasonably cheap and most convenient. They still use both a driver and a conductor on their buses. This is something that largely disappeared in the UK in the late 1960's. This is quite nostalgic for me as for one glorious year (it was the best job I ever had), in the middle of the 1960's, I worked as a bus conductor on the buses in Norwich. This said, we have, from time to time, used the local excursion boats and ferries to venture of the island to visit some of the other Greek islands that are close by...

Out and About

The Skiathos water taxi and Koukounaries beach

When on our sun beds on Troulos Bay beach we often see the water taxi coming or going between the resort of Koukounaries, to our right and the old port in Skiathos Town to our left. I often thought that one day we ought to try this unique form of holiday transport for ourselves. We never have to date. This is because the water taxi does not call and pick up or drop off on our beach. Anyway, the bus service is so very good that it would also be daft for us to travel to either Koukounaries or Skiathos Town by bus then catch the water taxi to the other harbour. If we did decide to do this at some point we would have to return to our resort on the bus anyway! Hey hoe who knows what can happen in the future, one day, someone might decide to include a stop for the water taxi at Troulos Bay beach to collect holidaymakers. If so people, us included, staying at Troulos Bay could then easily use the water taxi service for themselves...

Out and About

The monastery of Evangelistra and the Greek flag with orthodox priest's

It can be interesting, when you are on holiday, to visit religious sites as these locations often gives the visitor a tranquil, historical and interesting place to reflect in whilst enjoying your time in the summer sun. Found on the Island of Skiathos the monastery of Evangelistra has played an very important part in not just the islands history but also in the formation of the Greek nation and the Greek flag. In 1704 monks from Athos built the Evangelistria monastery on Skiathos. The Evangelistria monastery played a major part in the Greek War of Independence as a hide-out for Greek rebels. The first flag of Greece was created and hoisted in the Evangelistria monastery on Skiathos in 1807. Several prominent Greek military leaders (including Theodoros Kolokotronis and Andreas Miaoulis) had gathered there for consultation concerning an uprising, and they were sworn to this flag by the local bishop. Did you know that Skiathos can be translated as "the shadow of Athos"? Although Mount Athos, Greece's most famous Mountain (on the mainland far to the northeast of Skiathos), is usually hidden by summer haze, it can be seen on a clear spring and autumn day and on the mornings after a summer rain storm. The Athos peninsula is inhabited only by Greek Orthodox monks, who dwell in more than thirty picturesque medieval monasteries...

Out and About

Lalaria beach on the island of Skiathos

If you are thinking of visiting one of the north coast beaches of Skiathos it is useful to know that Lalaria beach is only available to be visited by boat. One way that you could visit here is to join one of the organised island boat trips that call here. They set sail from the old port in Skiathos Town. Or there are numerous yachts that can be hired on a daily rate basis. They can be found in the new port in Skiathos Town. You need to be aware however, that often when the wind is coming from the north and/or the sea is very rough the organised trips may not sail around the northern coastline. However, how you get there is one thing but Lalaria is famous for its crystal clear water and the natural rock sculpture that goes out to sea and is well worth a visit during your holiday…

Out and About

Kechria and Mandraki beaches on the north coast of the island

On the north coast of Skiathos Island, close to the airport, overlooking the sea and a popular tourist location for visitors is the old capital of the island Kastro. The long abandoned town has historical importance to the islanders as it was the ruined capital of the island. The islanders had made Kastro their capital to escape pirate attacks. Way back in 1207 the Gyzi brothers captured the island and built the Bourtzi, on an islet just out of Skiathos Town, to protect the capital from the pirates. But the Bourtzi was ineffective in protecting the population and in the mid-14th century the inhabitants moved the capital from the ancient site that lay where modern Skiathos Town is today to Kastro which is the Greek word for castle. They choose a located on a high rock, overlooking a steep cliff above the sea at the northernmost part of the island. After the War of Independence and demise of piracy in the Aegean, Kastro became less important as a strategic location and in 1830's, the island's capital was moved back to its original site where it still remains today. Also on north coast of the island is the beach of Kechria which has two beaches both with snack bars. It is quiet and secluded and usually un-crowded even at peek times of the year. Another beach on the north coast is at Aselinos. The beach is a long walk through countryside from the crossroads in Troulos village at bus stop (18). However it is also accessible by bike or jeep. It has a taverna and it usually has big waves. Many of the island boat trip stop here. You will find that a visit to Mandraki beach is well worth the effort but it can be a difficult journey by road. If you make the effort you will be rewarded by a long sandy beach that is quiet except in the high season. Be warned that there may be some nudity on the beach. It has however, a small taverna for that ice cold drink…

Out and About

Aghia Eleni and Koukounaries beaches

As we round the west coast of Skiathos we find Aghia Eleni Beach which is a long walk from the bus stop (25). It has a sandy beach with a snack bar however, it is worth the walk to witness the lovely sunsets that the west coast enjoys. Close by Banana Beach (big and little) bus stop (26) is a nudist beach with good water sport facilities and snack bars and of course great sunsets. As we round the west coast of Skiathos we start our journey down the south coast of the island and it's many beautiful sandy beaches. They can all be accessed easily by using the local bus. The first beach that we come to as we travel down the south coast is the fabulous beach resort of Koukounaries. This resort is world famous for having a long sandy beach, safe and gentile slopping seawater entry, edged by pine trees, a protected inshore lagoon, water sports and for being a great bucket and spade resort for all the family but it gets very busy throughout the summer season. There are good holidaymaker facilities on the beach and there are several snack bars along the beach. The little port at the eastern end of Koukounaries beach is well worth a visit as there and several local fishing boats tied up here which operate out of the harbour. The water taxi running between here and Skiathos old port is located here. The lagoon at the back of the beach is almost unique in the Greek islands. It is a long, broad expanse of brackish, jade-green water, linked to the sea by a narrow channel. On one side is a wide spread of reed beds and on the other side is a wildflower meadow that is colourful all the year round. It attracts dozens of butterflies and kingfishers and these can often be seen flying on or around the lake. Koukounaries beach, harbour and lagoon are all well worth a visit during your holiday to Skiathos…

Out and About

Troulos Bay beach and the Troulos Bay Hotel

As we make our way down the south coast from Koukounaries towards Skiathos Town the next beach we will visit call in on is Troulos Bay beach. When travelling by bus either from Koukounaries or from the town you will need to get off the bus at bus stop no. 20. Troulos Bay is also the resort that Susie and I base ourselves whenever we are holidaying on the island of Skiathos. Our hotel of choice for our stay is the Troulos Bay Hotel. The hotel is small and friendly with bags of facilities and a great sea view. It also benefits from having lots of very helpful and friendly staff. Troulos Bay has a golden sandy beach that shelves gently into the blue warm Mediterranean sea. There are also small craft, sunbeds with shades that are available to hire on the beach. Offshore is the small uninhabited island of Touranes and beyond that is the island of Evia (the second largest island in Greece). Troulos Bay beach also has the distinction of having a fresh water stream that flows right down to just behind the beachfront. The stream contains terrapins and freshwater fish. We, like many other holidaymakers, often go to visit the stream in the early morning to feed the terrapins and freshwater fish with small pieces of bread taken from our breakfast table…

Out and About

Poros, Kolios and Kanapitsa beaches on the south coast of Skiathos

As we reluctantly leave Troulos Bay beach and still heading south we will reach Poros beach that can be reached by boat or by getting off the local bus at bus stop no. 17. Progressing still further down the south coast is the beach of Agia Paraskevi which is accessed by boat or by local bus at bus stop no. 15. Here, like many others, the beach is a golden sandy beach and has safe seawater which is great for children and their buckets and spades. The same can be said for most of the beaches on the island of Skiathos. It has the customary taverna and/or snack bar with water sports available. Further still down the south coast is the beach of Kolios. Again accessed by boat or the local bus at bus stop no. 14. Kolios provides not just a great sandy beach and safe seawater but it also has a taverna, water sports and a beach bar. Still working our way down the south coast towards Skiathos Town is the beach at Kanapitsa which is reached from bus stop no. 13. Like just about all of the beaches featured it has water sports and a taverna as well as the customary sandy beach and safe seawater. Of course, whilst on holiday, you may decide to hire your own means of road or sea transport to travel from your accommodation to visit these wonderful beaches on the south coast of the island. You should note however, that many of the beaches on the north side of the island can only be visited by hiking overland or by boat!…

Out and About

The beaches at Tzaneria, Nostos and Achladias on the south coast

Continuing our journey down the south coast of the island of Skiathos we next come to the beaches of Tzaneria and Nostos. Again they too can be reached by boat or by bus at bus stop no. 12. As with the other beaches mentioned they both offer sunbeds, shades, sandy beaches, water sports, a diving school, tennis and a taverna. As we progress still further down the south coast we reach the resort of Achladias. The beach can be accessed by boat or getting of the bus at bus stop no. 10. This is very much a family friendly resort with a great beach that has lots of places to make sand castles and several good tavernas. You can also access the beach of Achladias by boat or from the same bus stop no. 10. As we begin to get ever closer to Skiathos Town we finish our beach hopping tour by calling into the beach at Megali Ammos. Again we can arrive by boat or the local bus at bus stop no. 6 or even by cycling/walking from the town as this is the first beach going south out of the Town of Skiathos. It has a narrow sandy beach and it is good for water sports. As we end our tour of some of the many great beaches on Skiathos it is worth noting that there are many more smaller beaches and coves that you can explore where you can often be the only people using it and have it all to yourselves. So as you set off to explore the beautiful holiday island of Skiathos by using your free map that you got from the airport or your tour representative or a shop/kiosk in town lets go! Remember you will need some form of sea or road transport or even a good pair of stout shoes as you set off around the island. I wish you well, good luck and enjoy!…

Out and About

The beaches at Platanias, Megas Gialos and Vromolimnos

Some of the sights you will be able to see when you are out and about on the island of Skiathos are the above vistas, but it should be remembered that before tourism, like many of the Greek islands, Skiathos was largely a fishing and agricultural community. One of the chief exports from the island was pine wood which grew abundantly on its hillsides but this had to cease after they nearly stripped the island of its wood. Luckily despite recent wild fires the trees are back and today tourism has taken over as the mainstay of the local economy…

Out and About

The skyline of Skiathos Town and the fine sandy beach at Troulos Bay

When on holiday, Susie and I visit Skiathos Town on several days and evenings during our stay on the island. When in town we often sit for hours watching people pass by the Mythos cafe and on and/or off the ferries come and going from the towns ferry port. The ferries are a vital and form a mainstay of the Greek islands transport network. The Greek people rely heavily on this form of transport for all their commerce and everyday needs. It is fascinating to watch all the different types of vehicles that come out or go into the belly of the ferry when it is in the docks of the ferry port in Skiathos Town. To be able to see and hear all the noise, hustle and bustle surrounding the port area whenever a ferry docks is truly absorbing and makes a great thing to watch. We like watching people going about their business or pleasure very much at home or when we are on holiday. Ferry and/or people watching in town makes a nice change of pace from being on the beach relaxing at Troulos Bay and watching the ferries passing leisurely by in the far distance either on there way to the mainland of Greece, other nearby islands or to Skiathos Town itself!...

Out and About

The hydrofoil leaving Skiathos ferry port and a ferry out at sea

When on holiday and looking to use the ferries it is important to know that the fastest means of ferry crossing is the hydrofoil or the "flying dolphin" which takes Skiathan's and visitors alike to such places as Skopelos, Alonnisos, Volos, Thessaloniki and Halkidiki. The much larger traditional ferries also call at many of these place and are relied upon for bringing in much of the fuel and provisions that the Skiathan's and tourists require. The ferry network is also very important in facilitating families and friends from both the Greek islands and the mainland of Greece to keep in physical contact with each other. Susie and I have not used the ferries during our stays on the island but we have taken some of the local boat trips to Skopelos and to several of the other Greek islands nearby. It was great fun to see other islands, different scenery and the friendly people during our two week holidays. Feature films have been made on these island in the past and there are today tours to see some of the settings for the blockbuster film that was called Mama Mia. This is a film that Susie and I love! So if you ,while on holiday, you feel adventurous get down to the Skiathos waterfront ports and get either a day trip or ferry ride to pastures anew but remember to come back to the paradise island of Skiathos at the end of the day to continue your holiday in paradise!...

Out and About

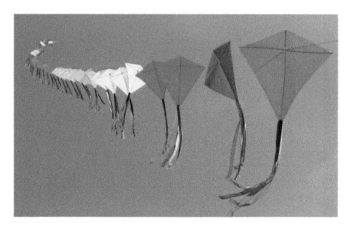

Kites flying high in the sky and it is always time for a cup of coffee

On all of our many holidays to the island of Skiathos we have gone out and about to enjoy the sights and sounds of the island we have always found time to regularly enjoy an ice cold frappe. As any Greek will tell you that you should always relax, don't hurry and find the time for a cup of coffee. This is also important when you are on holiday because relaxing, after all, this is why we all go on holiday in the first place! When we first visited Skiathos many years ago and we were out and about it was usual to see the local men sitting in the tavernas with a strong cup of coffee. They would also usually be playing the game backgammon whilst using their worry beads and drinking small cups of thick black coffee at anytime of the day or night. Sadly today the backgammon game board has largely been replaced by the handheld electronic devices/equipment and/or the internet mobile phone. Unlike in most of the UK where we have poor internet speeds all of the tavernas have free to their customers high speed internet connection. I think that this is sad really as much of the atmosphere has changed in the tavernas from the friendly banter of the board game to the tap/tapping of the keypad! Much like I am doing writing this today. All you share today is other peoples mobile phone chatter often made with raised voices. This is not good for the poor people trying to have a relaxing holiday like me having to grudgingly listen to other peoples moans and groans to people back home. Please turn the dam things OFF and enjoy the peace and quite of your holiday. As I get down off my soap box and slide it back under my chair. To finish this debate I must just say "hey hoe, I suppose, that's what some people would call progress". Sad really!...

Out and About

Agistri beach, a flag, and blue skies and a calm sea

Having been out and about and enjoyed the blue sky, the beaches and the wonderful views of the paradise Island of Skiathos we will, in the next chapter, put on our swimming costumes, kick off our flip-flops, take our sunglasses off, hold hands with the one you love, walk across the warm sand and enter what is for me one of the highlights of any summer holiday the sea! I, for one, feel great excitement as we leave the beach far behind us and venture out into the warm, clean, clear and wonderfully blue Mediterranean Sea. So lets go and enjoy the warm blue sea together…

Enjoying the Warm Blue Sea

Alan and Susie are all at sea at Troulos Bay

What a joy it is for us British travellers to be able to go into the warm, clean and blue Mediterranean sea and just float or swim safely. Coming from Norfolk where our local sea is called The North Sea. Its name is very apt because our North Sea is not only very cold, a dirty brown colour and has very strong undercurrents. All of which makes our North Sea very unattractive/unsafe to swim in. Therefore, one of our favourite things to do when we are on holiday in the Mediterranean is to go into the warm inviting sea off Troulos Bay. Personally I love to just float upright while turning myself 360 degrees whilst looking at the beach, the hotel, the hillside beyond then back to the sea, then at Touranes island, Evia and finally the mainland beyond. I can do this for ages. It is also an opportunity to watch the boats sail by while you are at their level. I love seeing all these things as I slowly turn around. I try and do this at least once on every day of our holiday to Skiathos…

Enjoying the Warm Blue Sea

Birds flying by at sunset, a starfish and the boat anchored in Troulos Bay

When we are on holiday at Troulos Bay I always take my snorkel equipment with me so I can enjoy not just what is above the sea but also view all the marvellous sea life that is under it! Also, from time to time, boats such as the one above decide to stop in at Troulos Bay and put their anchor down and stay for a while. The boat was owned by the chap who runs the boat hire and water sports concession on the beach so it would be there all summer long. Sadly in 2010 we noticed that the boats was no longer there. We later learnt that he had sold it! When we holiday now we miss seeing it bobbing up and down from our hotel balcony, hotel restaurant, our beach sunbed and when we are out swimming in the sea very much. Sad really…

Enjoying the Warm Blue Sea

A boat trip to Lalaria beach and the speedboat in Troulos Bay

On a recent holiday to Skiathos I was floating in the sea off Troulos Bay beach, as usual, when I noticed that the water sports man, even after disposing of his fishing boat, has remained hiring boats out on Troulos Bay beach. He spends his day, plying his trade, of hiring out speedboats and small day trip boats to help him earn a living. I have noticed, over the years, that he has a novel way of getting from the beach to his boats that are tied to buoys off shore in the bay. He uses an old surf board to ride out to retrieve whatever boat he requires. He leaves his surf board tied to the buoy where he gets the boat that he wants from then when the boat is returned he repeats this process but in reverse. I do not know what he does when more than one boat is hired at any one time? I guess he resorts to swimming out to the boat required! Some holidaymakers hire these boats out to explore the island but they often anchor in bays in many of the resorts for lunch and sunbathing. Some visitors however, join other holidaymakers on day trips around the island that leave from the old port in town. Featured above are one such organised boat trip and a picture of the speed boat that is owned by Yellis, one of the senior managers at the Troulos Bay Hotel. He anchors the boat in Troulos Bay throughout the summer season…

Enjoying the Warm Blue Sea

A loggerhead Turtle and the boat anchored in Troulos Bay

In 2008, whilst resting on my sunbed on Troulos Bay beach, after returning from a swim I noticed that the boat featured above which is the same one that was anchored in the Bay all summer long until 2010, was dazzling in the summer sun. As I sat on my sunbed at about 11.30 am so I took the picture of that boat, featured above (on the left), on the same day but at about 17.00 pm in the afternoon, this time sitting in the hotel poolside bar, I took the picture of the same boat, featured above (on the right). I think that these pictures demonstrate nicely why I like to take more than one picture of any given subject at different times of the day. This is because they show the different lighting effects on any given subject which is dependant on the changing weather conditions and the time of the day that the picture is taken…

Enjoying the Warm Blue Sea

fishing boat at Koukounaries and a fishing boat passing by

When enjoying the sea on holiday on Skiathos often it is the things that float on the sea that is most interesting! This was apparent when Susie and I, one day in 2011, decided that we would spend the morning in the beach resort of Koukounaries. So we walked up the lane from our hotel and caught the local bus at bus stop 20. We got off at bus stop 22 then walked down the lane that runs beside the lagoon which leads to the small Koukounaries fishing harbour. This was a very pleasant stroll and after spending some time watching the ducks swimming under the walkway bridge between the beach and the harbour. We then walked around the harbour walls. As we did we admired the local fishing boats that were being made ready, by the fishermen, for their evening/night time fishing trip. Later that same day, in the early evening, back at our hotel and sitting on our balcony looking out to sea we noticed those same fishing boats that came bob, bob, bobbing by our bay on the way to their fishing grounds. What a lovely sight they made and we wished them a good nights fishing!...

Enjoying the Warm Blue Sea

Floats going out to sea at Troulos Bay and wild plants on Koukounaries beach

Like many other people being by the seaside is an important part of why we choose the holiday destination that we do. Being able to enjoy swimming in the sea is also high on our priority list. This is why we usually have our summer holiday on the Greek island of Skiathos. Another of our holiday traditions is that on most days Susie and I try to go for an early morning walk on the beach. We love looking out to sea and watching the skies gradually brighten to herald the start of yet another day in paradise. We also love beach-combing and looking for small pretty shells, shiny pebbles and/or anything else that may be small and interesting that has been washed up onto the shoreline overnight. Anything we find we call our treasure and take it home to the UK as a reminder of all the happy times that we have had on the beach. Back home, we have, to date filled two deep glass jars with these treasured keepsakes. We have, over the years, always beach-combed and have collected many interesting items from all of the beaches that we have visited. Both in the UK and abroad. The glass jars are displayed in our bathroom and they bring us great joy because each time we look at them they remind us of happy times and invoke all the precious memories of our wonderful holidays by the sea…

Enjoying the Warm Blue Sea

The statue in Skiathos Town old port and the beach at Kechria

Susie and I not only enjoy being beside the seaside when we are at our hotel and/or on the beach at Troulos Bay but also when we go into Skiathos Town. When we are in town we often visit the Bakaliko restaurant where Bello is head chief (he is our hotels head waiter Ervin's brother). When there we always sit at one of the seafront tables that are located on a platform that extends out over the sea in the bay of Skiathos Town. We like to look out at all of the local fishing boats and yachts that are anchor off shore in the bay. I often ask Susie to take a photograph (snap) of an individual or group of boats (her camera has a better telephoto lens on it for such snaps than my camera has). I use these snaps, when we get back home, as visual aids to inspire and remind me of our holiday when doing a watercolour painting(s) back in the UK. I will often bring one or more of these paintings, framed up, when we go back on holiday to the island the following year. These I give as gifts to one/or more of our Skiathan friend(s)…

Enjoying the Warm Blue Sea

Marble being queried and all alone on Troulos Bay beach

When I am rotating around in the warm blue sea at Troulos Bay I often marvel at the ever decreasing Greek mainland mountainside off to my left as I rotate clockwise around in the sea. What I am actually looking at is the extraction of marble taking place before my very eyes! Marble is a very popular building material in Greece and further afield and obviously the marble stone needs to be quarried from somewhere. This process of marble extraction, in action, is seen in the white chopped out areas on the Greek mainland mountain surface in the above picture. However, the lone lady, in the lower picture, may well also be looking at the quarry from Troulos Bay beach or more likely just enjoying the general view of the blue sea of the Mediterranean or even something else entirely. Who Knows! If you holiday on the island of Skiathos and take the water taxi from the old port or Koukounaries or any of the other boat trips that goes up/down the south coast of the island of Skiathos you will see, for yourselves, another working marble quarry site on the hillside of Skiathos Island itself…

Enjoying the Warm Blue Sea

Dolphins leaping off Troulos Bay and the "Lazy Days" boat trip

While holidaying on the island of Skiathos in 2008 we were lucky enough to go on the "Lazy Days" boat trip that ran from Koukounaries harbour, stopping in at Troulos Bay beach before spending the whole day cruising around the island and visiting beaches both on Skiathos itself and some of the other small islands nearby. Susie and I had a great day out with the lovely Skiathan family that operated the trip but unfortunately they could not get enough passengers to join them each day that year and had to sell their precious boat at the end of that season. We are very sad that we and others will no longer be able to join them for this great day out in the future to enjoy the warm blue sea and all the fantastic scenery this trip enabled us to witness!…

Enjoying the Warm Blue Sea

The boat at anchor and a yacht sailing past Troulos Bay

One of the real pleasures of lying on my sun bed on Troulos Bay beach and looking out to sea is that you get to see a large range of different sailing craft passing by. These range from very small boats to large boats like the ferries, cruise ships and tankers and everything in between. The sea between Evia and Troulos Bay on Skiathos is very busy with many craft passing by the bay everyday. Thankfully these sea views continue for us even when we are in the hotel restaurant having a meal or when we are sitting on our hotel room balcony enjoying a quite drink. This is because they both have superb sea views. This adds so much to our holiday and is the main reason why we selected The Troulos Bay Hotel as our holiday accommodation of choice in the first place. There is something quite restful and relaxing about watching a sailing boat making its way passed our vantage points. The yacht pictured above is seen passing Troulos Bay and is probably heading towards the yacht marina at the new port in Skiathos Town and is coming from the direction of Koukounaries…

Enjoying the Warm Blue Sea

A island flower and a rainbow over Troulos Bay and into the warm blue sea

Troulos Bay on the Island of Skiathos really is the place where you will find that pot of gold at the end of the rainbow. When you do it is usually falling into the warm blue sea! When you are on holiday you should always try to enjoy your time by the sea to the full! If you have seen the film Mamma Mia you will undoubtedly remember the dance sequence performed on a wooden jetty out over the warm Mediterranean Sea. Now that is people enjoying themselves! Whilst it is true that the sequence was filmed on an island nearby there are still several wooden jetties that you will encounter in many of the resorts on the island of Skiathos. So don't be shy and if you find one just get up there on the jetty and dance the day away. Or if you are a bit shy why not wait until dusk and do your dancing then! But be careful diving off the jetty into the sea as the sea may not be as deep as you may think! For those of you that really want to dive into the sea off a wooden stage in private then get yourself to the end of the Bourtzi in Skiathos Town. There you can go down the steps to the diving board situated there and enjoy the warm blue sea to your hearts content. Remember however, to be very careful to watch out for the local children who may be there and may have already dived in before you!…

Enjoying the Warm Blue Sea

A gull, Alan all at sea and a ferry leaving Skiathos Town ferry port

By holidaying by the sea on Skiathos you often get the opportunity to watch the boats go by from the shore however, as already mentioned, it is fascinating to watch the ferries coming and going from the ferry port in Skiathos Town. One of the best memories I have of this is when Susie and I were sitting on a bench at the front of the Bourtzi in 2012. We were watching hundreds of motor bikes come roaring off the ferry. The noise was incredible. That week-end they toured and roared around the island for a few days having fun before re-boarding the ferries to go back over to the mainland. It was a fantastic sight and apparently the Greek bikers club visit a different Greek island every year so who knows you may be lucky enough to see them at a resort near you real soon!…

Enjoying the Warm Blue Sea

A loggerhead turtle and Alan in the warm sea at Troulos Bay

I have already mentioned the water taxi but it is worth revisiting this form of transport as it really gets you up and close with the warm blue sea. It is a much quieter form of sea transport than the ferries and slower so you get the chance to enjoy the views. The water taxis runs from the old port to various south coast resorts up as far as Koukounaries. We have never, as yet, used the water taxis ourselves because it does not call in at Troulos Bay but should they decide to include stopping in at our resort in the future we would undoubtedly use it to get into town from time to time. It must be nice to be cruising down the coast and drinking in all of the fabulous views of the island seen from a different perspective. Remember to look out for the marble quarry as you glide down the south coast of the island of Skiathos…

Enjoying the Warm Blue Sea

Susie on the Lazy Days boat trip and a Greek Island church

When on holiday on the Island of Skiathos it is always a good idea to take a boat trip so you can get a feel for the island by cruising by it's coastline on the warm blue sea. Susie and I have usually managed at least one boat trip per holiday to the island. I have already mentioned one such boat trip that we have been on that was called the "Lazy Days" earlier in this chapter. Susie and I enjoyed this trip onboard very much. In the top picture note the lack of fellow passengers which ultimately led to the cancellation of any future Lazy days boat trips and ultimately forced the owners to sell their beloved boat. The trip however, was great at the time. The sun shone down on the few of us on the boat, the sea was calm and blue and even though we can not go on this trip in the future we were lucky enough to have had the experience and enjoyment at that time in the past. Oh those were such Happy Days sailing on the warm blue sea!…

Enjoying the Warm Blue Sea

Troulos Bay beach from the deck of the lazy days boat trip

When you are holidaying on the Island of Skiathos it would be never more enjoyable then to be either in or on the warm blue sea. I have enjoyed every moment when I have been snorkeling in the clear warm blue seawater . I was lucky enough to not only see countless different types of fish but also starfish, jelly fish (not so good) and of better still octopus. Even when we were floating on the surface of the sea we had great views. We often watched sailing vessels, saw distant islands, the mainland of Greece, marble quarries, aircraft in the blue sky and once we were even lucky enough to see three dolphins gliding past! I. Like many others, have also inadvertently step or even fell into the sea. Luckily unlike back home in the UK the sea off Skiathos is lovely and warm. One example of me stepping/failing into the sea also accompanies the pictures above that were taken as we cruised back from our "Lazy Days" boat trip. The pictures show the Troulos Bay beach and the Troulos Bay Hotel beyond. Whilst disembarking from the boat disaster struck: I remember stepping down off the gangplank of the boat just at the wrong time and stepping straight into the sea up to my knees. But even this could not spoil (or dampen) what had been a great day out. This was mainly because I had, very sensibly, worn shorts and flip-flops (I think Susie suggested that I did so) for our day out and so, for me, getting wet was no big problem at all and did not spoil our day out on the warm blue sea…

Enjoying the Warm Blue Sea

Sunset over the island of Evia and fishing boats in Skiathos Town bay

When you are enjoying the warm blue sea on the Island of Skiathos and spot something that is interesting to you is the time when you need to have remembered to bring your camera or mobile phone with you to enable you to capture that moment. Susie and I always add to the fun by having our own photographic competition when on holiday to see who can get the best image of our holiday. Susie, as usual, won our photography competition in 2014 with the above picture of fishing boats in Skiathos Town Bay. She took the picture from the Bakaliko restaurant platform at dusk hence the lovely light and reflections on the fishing boats. The picture also leads us very nicely into the next chapter of this book where we will venture into the must do of your holiday to Skiathos and that is exploring Skiathos Town by night...

Exploring Skiathos Town at Night

Landed
Plane with its
Lights on…

Skiathos
Airport in the
dark…

Skiathos
Town at night
Illuminated…

One thing to know about Skiathos is that flights are allowed into the islands airport after dusk so there is no aircraft noise to disturb the peace in Skiathos Town during the evening and at night. This leaves only the loud music from the bars and clubs to disturb the peace! We think that Skiathos Town at night is a truly magical place. The busy atmosphere of the day gives way to a more relaxed environment where tourists and locals alike parade up and down the promenades of the old port, Bourtzi and the new port. They wear their best outfits or in the case of us UK visitors that wear shorts with a brightly coloured tee shirt and the mandatory flip-flops. We love wandering around the waterfront and the narrow streets of the town. Susie loves to have time to look in the many tourist shops up the main street in town. We sometimes have a meal or just a drink along the way to keep us going until it is time to catch the bus back to the Troulos Bay Hotel. There we will have a drink in the hotel lounge bar with the hotel manager George and a chat before retiring to our room and balcony for a good night cup of tea and/or coffee to toast another great day of our holiday in paradise…

Exploring Skiathos Town at Night

Moonlight on Skiathos bay and Alan eating out in the old port at night

One of the real joys of having a holiday on the island of Skiathos and spending sometime in the evening in Skiathos Town is the opportunity it gives you to eat outside in a vibrant and happy environment. Eating out in the evening air is one of the joys of a Mediterranean holiday and something that we can rarely do back home in the UK. The Greeks tend to eat their evening meal late at about 9.30 pm or later but like most British visitors Susie and I prefer to eat at about 8 pm . This means that often there are plenty of choice as to where to eat. Often we select the restaurant with the best views of the town or harbour for our evening meal. This is also the criteria we use when deciding where to have our lunchtime meals when we are in town during the day. The Greek food is fantastic and would suggest you try the local dishes and not just stick to the traditional tourist fare. I believe you will be pleasantly surprised at how tasty real authentic Greek food can be. In town and throughout the rest of the island you may have to shop around somewhat to find tavernas and/or restaurants that not just cater for the tourists with fast foods such as pizza, steak and chips with everything but also offers more traditional foods such as moussaka or Kleftiko on their menus!…

Exploring Skiathos Town at Night

Skiathos Town at dusk and shopping in Skiathos Town at Night

When you are in Skiathos Town at dusk the main shopping street begins to take on a whole new atmosphere. People begin to emerge from their early evening siesta to wander around among the bright lights. They often just window shop but many go into the tourist gift shops looking for that gift to take home to remind them of their stay on the island. The shops are mainly up the main street and are full of tourist type goods. You can find almost anything to suit your budget to take home as a keepsake or to give as a gift to a loved one. When you are wandering around town there is a plethora of fast food, more traditional tavernas and good restaurants to spend some time in and rest your weary legs. After just perhaps a refreshing cold drink or a snack or even after a main meal it is back to the task of shopping. It is hard work but someone has to do it and shopping when on holiday has become a traditional activity for many holidaymakers. You will also see and be able to interact with the locals who you will find to be very approachable and friendly…

Exploring Skiathos Town at Night

The main shopping street in town during the day

Skiathos Town is not just there to be enjoyed in the evening but is also a vibrant and interesting place to be during the day. Susie and I love wandering up and down the shopping street during the day or in the early evening. Often Susie will go into every shop to browse while I stand about outside and people watch, enjoying the ambience. I do this, you realise, just to rest my poorly knees, you understand and not because I do not enjoy shopping. I do however, go into some of the shops to help Susie choose some of the gifts that we want to take home. Ever year for example we manage to find a new fridge magnet for our fridge back in the UK as well as the odd bits and pieces to take back for our friends and family. We however, to be honest, find that more often than not we get things for ourselves. One good thing about this street is that there are plenty of bars and cafes that you can take a break from shopping in and have a drink before making some more progress up the street. In the pictures above you will see that the Skiathos Town shopping street is not always packed with tourists. These are the times when I prefer to go shopping however, Susie prefers the street when it is bustling with holidaymakers and local people!…

Exploring Skiathos Town at Night

A restaurant and a taverna on the main shopping street in Skiathos Town

When you are exploring Skiathos Town at night and you are wandering up and/or down the main shopping street it is worth going down some of the side streets or alleys that lead off the main thoroughfare as well. This is because there are often some shops tucked away down these side streets. Another advantage of wandering of the main shopping street is that there are countless tavernas and restaurants situated down almost every side street and alley. This you may find, as we did, useful, as often the price for a drink or a meal you pay in these, can sometimes be significantly lower than you would pay in the main tourist parts of town. We found that the prices for food and drink that we paid in the waterfront tavernas and restaurants and the ones up the main shopping street were indeed higher than in the side streets but remember you are paying extra for the views that they give you and not just for the food and drink! We often choose to have our meals and drinks on the waterfront and pay that little bit more for this very reason. Remember you are on holiday after all!…

Exploring Skiathos Town at Night

The old port and new port in the evening

When you are in town in the daytime or in the evening and walking along the promenade in the old port in Skiathos Town you will see some broad steps leading up past a bar just before the children's play area on your right. Go up these steps which will take you to the main town plaza where the church Trion Lerarchon stands to your right. It has a tall clock tower to the front and is really beautiful inside. In the evening it is all lit up and looks magnificent and is well worth a visit either during the day or in the evening. We have wandered around this plaza several times during our holidays to the island and we have enjoyed the atmosphere of the location. There are several tavernas and shops close by including a great bakery that has lovely cakes and other bakery items for sale…

Exploring Skiathos Town at Night

The windmill restaurant on the hill and the new port at night

Leading off from the church plaza featured on the previous page you can venture down any the streets or alleys that you like to your right and you will pass a few shops and eventually you will reach the main shopping street. If however, you turn left in the plaza and go past several well appointed restaurants then up some more steps you will find even more fine eating establishments. We have made this climb several times and the view from their balconies are amazing, especially at night and is well worth the climb but whether you will be able to find a seat in these restaurants could be another matter so perhaps you should pre-book a table before making the climb!…

Exploring Skiathos Town at Night

A yacht, Susie, the port, Lynn, Andy and a taverna cat

One of the joys of being on holiday is that very quickly you find the places that you enjoy the most. One such places that we enjoy visiting when we are in Skiathos Town at night is the Bakaliko restaurant located on the seafront of the bay. This is because that from the vantage point of our table on the raised platform of the Bakaliko restaurant we can look out over the new port and the town which at night is all lit up. It is truly worth getting a table along the bay front to see this sight at least on one evening during your holiday. We always try to go and see Bello, the head chef of the restaurant, at least one evening during our holiday and in recent years we have also been accompanied by our good friends Andrew and Lynn as they also enjoy the food that Bello prepares and cooks. In recent years, we have also had a meal here on Susie's birthday evening as we are on holiday on the island at the same time. The staff and Bello have always help make this a special night for us by presenting Susie with a birthday celebratory drink. They also join in with us in singing happy birthday to her which she always finds embarrassing!…

Exploring Skiathos Town at Night

The bay and a cat in Skiathos Town at night

Susie and I always find the time when we are out strolling around Skiathos Town in the evening to take a walk around the Bourtzi and look at the old port all lit up. As we go further around the Bourtzi we get a view out to sea and then finally the ferry port with the new port area beyond. These are also fully illuminated. Sometimes, as it is usually warm in the evenings, it is worth sitting down on one of the benches provided all the way around the Bourtzi and just let the atmosphere wash over you and enjoy the moment remember after all you are on holiday!…

Exploring Skiathos Town at Night

Skiathos Town old port all aglow at night

When you are out and about in Skiathos Town at night one of the best sights you can be greeted by when you stroll around the Bourtzi is the free light show. Here you will see the town lighting reflected in the sea. It is one of the reasons why we like wandering around town in the evening and it is beautiful. What could be nicer than to be able to stroll around in short sleeve shirts or tee-shirt and shorts on a warm summer's night with the one you love and enjoy the free light show of the new port, bay, Bourtzi, old port and town! Of course it helps that the night is still young and full of possibilities and/or opportunities! So let us just stroll a bit more and then decide where we are going to eat tonight!…

Exploring Skiathos Town at Night

The old port and the moon comes out to play over Skiathos Town

When you are exploring Skiathos Town at night you will find that the old port, when lit up, is a magical place. It is best seen if you either taking a walk onto the Bourtzi (already described earlier) or you can take a walk down to the far end of the promenade past the fishing boats and look back at the old port from there. Either way you will be greeted by one of the best views the island has to offer. We often have an early evening drink with our friends George and Eve at the Mythos Cafe that is right on the old port waterfront before setting out for a stroll or some shopping before finding somewhere great to have our evening meal. This really is what holidays are all about…

Exploring Skiathos Town at Night

The new port, Alan at the Lo&La restaurant and boats in Skiathos Bay

When we have been either on the Bourtzi or to the old port we often have a sit on the benches beside the ferry port entrance and people watch for a little while during the evening. The local children will be sitting on a curb along the promenade selling pretty shells or necklaces for some extra pocket money or just laughing and playing together. Their parents are often close at hand and would be quick to reprimand any bad behaviour from them. Something parents back in the UK could well do with copying! The good natured, happy smiles and relaxing atmosphere this creates makes Skiathos Town a pleasant place to spend a hot summers evening in. So you can just relax and wander around the town maybe, stopping to have a drink or a very good meal and generally enjoying your holiday to the full!...

Exploring Skiathos Town at Night

Moonlight on Skiathos and Susie in the Lo & La restaurant

When we have been exploring Skiathos Town at night we have noticed that away from the main shopping street you can often be the only people that are about during the early evening. I guess this is because the locals are indoors resting whilst the holiday makers are still having their showers after another hard day on the beach. As time moves on and the evening gets a bit later the number of people out and about has grown and again the atmosphere changes from quiet and relaxed to chatty, noisy and bustling excitement. After we have had our evening meal, had a stroll and done any shopping that we have wanted to do it is often the time that Susie and I decide to wander back to the bus station and catch the bus back to Troulos Bay Hotel for the night. We can then enjoy a night cap with George the hotel manager in the hotel lounge bar before going up to bed at the end of another brilliant day of our holiday on the paradise island of Skiathos…

Exploring Skiathos Town at Night

The Windmill restaurant in town and the Troulos Bay Hotel

When exploring Skiathos Town the Windmill restaurant can be seen both day and night as it is perched right on the highest point of Skiathos Town opposite the bus station. People say that they have had a good meal there however, Susie and I have only managed to struggle up there once (my poorly knees you know). That was also during the day and when we eventually reach it had only just opened and the young girl who obviously worked there was not interested in starting work anytime soon. Thirsty and disappointed we left and struggled back down the very steep steps and alleys back to the waterfront. Needless to say we have not been back up there since. I am sure we were just unlucky and the Windmill restaurant is great most of the time! Having exhausted ourselves it is now time to Skiathos Town by night and return to our beautiful hotel. When we have been talking to our Skiathan friends they have told us much about their beliefs, customs and culture. In the next chapter we will be sharing some of these many traditions and customs of the people of Greece with you…

Understanding Greek Traditions

Greek traditional dancers and the Parthenon of Athens

Susie and I have spent many a happy summer holiday on one or other of the many Greek Islands. We have also been lucky enough to have visited many of the important ancient sites and cities on the mainland of Greece over the last twenty years. During our holidays to Greece we have met and befriended many of the local Greek people. Our Greek hosts have, over the years, told us many interesting facts about Greece, its customs and its people. We have found these facts very interesting and enlightening. They help to explain many of things about the ways of the Greeks that we did not understand. I have therefore, included these facts in the pages that follow so you too can begin to understand the traditions of the Greek people. To help us understand the culture and beliefs that have driven the traditions of the Greek people we will start by leaning something about their past. Almost since time began Greece has been recognised as the birthplace of civilisation and democracy. Athens is one of the oldest cities in Europe. Greece and Athens in particular is also seen as the birthplace of democracy, Western philosophy, the Olympic Games, political science, Western literature, historiography, major mathematical principles, and Western theories of tragedy and comedy. Greece has given to the world its Gods of Mythology, the ancient Olympic Games, The Parthenon, Minoan Culture and much, much more. In more recent times it has been the country of choice for a vast number of visitors (tourists) both to see its ancient cultural heritage sites, its cities and to holiday on one of its multitude of beautiful paradise Islands. Greece has an abundance of fabulous sandy beaches, rugged scenery and a very warm, welcoming and friendly people…

Understanding Greek Traditions

The Greek people will always find the time for a coffee.

Greece has an area of 50,949 square miles (131,958 square kilometres), Greece is roughly the size of Alabama. The population of Greece is more than 10 million people.

Greece attracts approximately 16.5 million tourists each year which is more than the country's entire population. Tourism constitutes nearly 16% of the Gross Domestic Product (GDP) of Greece.

In Greece everyone has to vote. Voting is required by law for every citizen who is 18 years of age or older.

Greece has more international airports than most other countries in the world. This is because there are so many foreign tourists that want to visit its shores.

Greece is the world's third leading producer of olives. The Greeks have cultivated olive trees since ancient times. Some olive trees planted in the thirteenth century are still producing olives today.

Greece has zero navigable rivers this is because of the mountainous terrain. Nearly 80% of Greece is mountainous.

In Greece approximately 98% of the people are ethnic Greeks. Turks form the largest minority group. Other minorities are Albanians, Macedonians, Bulgarians, Armenians, and gypsies. 12 million people around the world speak Greek. They live mostly in Greece, Cyprus, Italy, Albania, Turkey and the United States of America, among other countries.

Thousands of English words come from the Greek language, sometimes via the Roman adaptation into Latin and then into English. Common English words from Greek include "academy," "apology," "marathon," "siren," "alphabet," and "typhoon."…

Understanding Greek Traditions

An old Greek legend says that when God created the world, he sifted all the soil onto the earth through a strainer. After every country had good soil, he tossed the stones left in the strainer over his shoulder and that is what created Greece. Greece has more than 2,000 islands, of which approximately 170 are populated. Greece's largest island is Crete (3,189 sq. miles) (8,260 sq. km.).

Over 40% of the population of Greece lives in the capital Athens (*Athina* in Greek). Since becoming the capital of modern Greece, its population has risen from 10,000 in 1834 to 3.6 million in 2001. Greece has been continuously inhabited for more than 7,000 years.

Greece enjoys more than 250 days of sunshine each year which means that they have 3,000 hours of sun every year.

Greek Men currently, must serve from one year to 18 months in a branch of the counties armed forces. The government spends 6% of the annual Gross Domestic Product (GDP) on the military.

Ancient Greece was not a single country like modern day Greece. Rather, it was made up of about 1,500 different city-states or *poleis* (singular, *polis*). Each had its own laws and army, and they often quarrelled and waged war on one another. Athens was the largest city-state.

Life expectancy in Greece currently the life expectancy for Greek females is 82 years and for men, 77 years. Greece is ranked 26th in the world for life expectancy rates.

Greece is the leading producer of sea sponges in the world…

Understanding Greek Traditions

Football is the national sport of Greece.

Greek merchant ships make up 70% of the European Union's total merchant fleet. According to Greek law, 75% of a ship's crew must be Greek.

Retirement homes are rare in Greece. Grandparents usually live with their children's family until they die. Most young people live with their families until they marry.

Greek structures such as doors, windowsills, furniture, and church domes are painted a turquoise blue, especially in the Cyclades Islands. It is used because of an ancient belief that this shade of blue keeps evil away.

Feta cheese which is made from goat's milk is the Greek's national cheese and dates back to the Homeric ages. The average per-capita consumption of feta cheese in Greece is the highest in the world.

In Greece people celebrate the "name day" of the saint that bears their name rather than their own birthday.

Thousands of birds stop in Greece's wetlands on their migrations. As many as 100,000 birds from northern Europe and Asia spend their winters there.

People say that "taking the bull by its horns" comes from the Greek myth of Hercules saving Crete from a raging bull by seizing its horns. It may also come from the myth of bull leaping of the Minions.

The first Olympic Games took place in 776 B.C. The first Greek Olympic champion was a Greek cook named Coroebus who won the sprint race. The tradition of lighting the Olympic torch before the start of the games goes right back to the earliest days of the Olympic games…

Understanding Greek Traditions

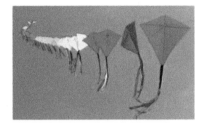  

A long-standing dispute between Britain and Greece concerns the Elgin Marbles (the Greeks prefer to call them the Parthenon Marbles), which are housed in a London museum. The British government believes that it acquired them fairly through its purchase from Lord Elgin, while the Greeks claim the purchase was illegal as the marbles were the property of the Greek people and therefore, stolen.

Greece has one of the richest diversities of wildlife in Europe, including 116 species of mammals, 18 amphibians, 59 reptiles, 240 birds, and 107 fish. However, sadly about half of the endemic mammal species are currently in danger of becoming extinct.

The Monk Seal has long been a part of Greek's natural and cultural heritage and is described in **The Odyssey**. The head of a monk seal was even found on a Greek coin dated 500 BC.

Greece organised the first municipal rubbish/waste dump in the Western world in around 500 B.C. Slaves made up between 40% and 80% of ancient Greece's population. Slaves were captives from wars, abandoned children, or children of slaves.

In the 2nd World War during the Nazi occupation of Greece in WWII, most Jews were taken to concentration camps across Europe. The Jewish population in Greece fell sharply from 78,000 to less than 13,000 by the end of the war.

In Greece the dead are always buried because the Greek Orthodox Church forbids cremation. Five years after a burial, the body is exhumed and the bones are first washed with wine and then placed in a building called an ossuary. This is done in part to relieve the shortage of land available in Greek cemeteries.

Government corruption cost Greece about $1 billion in 2009. Currently Greece's national debt is larger than the country's economy. Its credit rating, or its perceived ability to repay its debts, is the lowest in the euro zone.

The Greek language has been spoken for more than 3,000 years, making it one of the oldest languages in Europe…

Understanding Greek Traditions

Greeks do not wave with an open hand. In fact, it is considered an insult to show the palm of the hand with the fingers extended. Greeks wave with the palm closed. **After giving a** compliment Greeks make a puff of breath through pursed lips, as if spitting. This is meant to protect the person receiving the compliment from the "evil eye".

No point in Greece is more than 85 miles (137 kilometres) from seawater. Greece has about 9,000 miles of coastline, the 10th longest coastline in the world.

Greece was once a mass of rock that was completely underwater. When a tectonic plate crashed into Europe, the collision raised the sea bed and created Greece's mountain ranges. The plate is still moving and causes earthquakes and tremors all around the Aegean most years.

Greek soldiers (hoplites) in ancient Greece wore up to 70 pounds (33 kilograms) of bronze armour.

The ancient Greeks are often called the inventors of mathematics because they were the first to make it a theoretical discipline. The work of Greek mathematicians such as Pythagoras, Euclid, Archimedes, and Apollonius lies at the basis of modern mathematics. The first Greek philosopher is considered to be Thales of Miletus (c. 624-546 B.C.). He was the first to give a natural explanation of the origin of the world rather than a mythological one.

The Peloponnesian War (431 - 404 BC) between Athens and the Peloponnesian League led by Sparta left ancient Greece in ruins and marked the end of the golden age of Greece.

A Greek Spartan speciality was a black soup made from salt, vinegar, and blood. No one in the rest of Greece would drink it…

Understanding Greek Traditions

The first Greek tragedy was performed in 534 B.C. It was staged by a priest of Dionysus named Thespis. He also wrote and performed a part separate from the traditional tragic chorus, which also designated him as the first known actor. In fact, the word "thespian" (actor) derives from his name.

The British poet Lord Byron (1788 - 1824) was so enamoured with the Greeks that he travelled to Greece to fight against the Turks in the Greek War of Independence. He contracted a fever there and died at the age of 36. The Greeks consider him a national hero.

The word "barbarian" comes from Greek barbaroi, which means people who do not speak Greek and therefore sound like they're saying "bar-bar-bar-bar." So I guess that makes me and the rest of us from the UK barbarians!

In ancient Greece one of the dishes enjoyed by ancient Greek men at feasts was roast pig stuffed with thrushes, ducks, eggs, and oysters. Most feasts were for men only, though there were female entertainers (this was not considered a respectable occupation for a women).

Pre-Socratic Greek philosopher Anaximander (c. 610-546 B.C.) is credited with writing the first philosophical treatise and making the first map of the known world. He is also considered to be the first scientist who recorded a scientific experiment.

Greek Spartan warriors were known for their long, flowing hair. Before a battle, they would carefully comb it. Cowardly soldiers would have half their hair and half their beards shaved off.

Ostracism allowed Athenian citizens to temporarily exile people who were thought dangerous to the public. If it was voted that ostracism was necessary, each citizen inscribed a name on a piece of pottery or ostracon in a secret ballet. The person who had his/her names on the most pieces of pottery had to leave Athens within 10 days for 10 years…

Understanding Greek Traditions

Only Greek boys and men were actors in ancient Greek plays. They wore large masks so audience members could see what part they were playing. Theatre staff carried big sticks to control the audience because sometimes the huge audiences would get over excited by a play and would riot.

The Greeks in ancient times, would sacrifice one hundred bulls to Zeus during each Olympic Games.

The Greeks revolutionised the art of sculpture. Instead of stiff poses and blank faces, Greek artists began to carve statues of people that showed both movement and emotion.

The Greek Temple of Artemis was built on the site of two earlier shrines dating back as far as the eight century B.C. Now in modern-day Turkey, it was one of the Seven Wonders of the Ancient World. It was built around 550 B.C. and was destroyed in 356 B.C. by Herostratus.

The Parthenon (Place of the Partheons, from parthenos or "virgin") was built almost 2,500 years ago and sits on the Acropolis above the city of Athens. It actually featured colourful sculptures and a large gold-and-ivory statue of Athena. It took 15 years to build.

The ancestors of the Greeks were Indo-Europeans who entered Greece around 1900 B.C. They lived alongside the Minoans for many centuries before giving rise to the Mycenaean civilization which ended abruptly in the twelfth century B.C. After a "dark ages" of 300 years in which the knowledge of writing was lost, Greece gave birth to one of the most influential civilisation the world has ever known which we call Classical Greece.

By law the only people eligible for citizenship in Sparta were direct descendants of the original Doric settlers. Because of this, there were never more than about 6,000-7,000 male citizens in Sparta, compared with up to 40,000 in Athens…

Understanding Greek Traditions

Greek's highest elevation is the legendary home of Zeus and other Olympian gods and goddesses, Mount Olympus at 9,750 feet (2,917 meters). Its lowest elevation is the Mediterranean Sea, or sea level.

Alexander the Great was the first Greek ruler to put his own face on Greek coins. Previously, Greek coins had shown the face of a god or goddess.

The word "tragedy" is Greek for "goat-song" because early Greek tragedies honoured Dionysus, the god of wine, and the players wore goatskins. Tragedies were noble stories of gods, kings, and heroes. Comedy or "revel," on the other hand, were about lower-class characters and their antics.

The most famous modern writer in Greece is Nikos Kazantzakis (1883-1957). His novels **Zorba the Greek** and **The Last Temptation of Christ** were both made into movies, though the Greek Orthodox Church expelled him from their religion for writing **The Last Temptation of Christ**.

Greece's official name is the Hellenic Republic. It is also known as Ellas or Ellada. The Greek flag includes nine blue-and-white horizontal stripes, which some scholars say stand for the nine syllables of the Greek motto "Eleftheria i Thanatos" or "Freedom or Death." Blue represents Greece's sea and sky, while white stands for the purity of the struggle of freedom. In the upper left-hand corner is the traditional Greek Orthodox cross.

Greece has two major political parties: the Socialists (Panhellenic Socialists Movements or PASOK) and the Democrats (the New Democracy Party). Both were founded in 1974 after Greece's military dictatorship collapsed.

Greece has one of the lowest divorce rates in the EU (4.8% in 2016). Greece traditionally also has the highest abortion rates. About 10% of a Greek worker's pay is taken for taxes and another 10% for national health care in return the government provides free hospital treatment and other medical services. Greek workers currently receive at least one months paid holiday/vacation every year…

Understanding Greek Traditions

Anyone who has visited Greece will be well aware of the numerous small roadside shrines (see above) that often contain lit candles and vases of dried flowers. These are erected at sites where loved ones have had a tragic accident, often fatal and their family leave them a light to remember them by.

Greece's previous currency the drachma, was 2,650 years old and was Europe's oldest currency. The drachma was replaced by the Euro in 2002.

Throughout history the Greeks have loved the sea. They have more than 1,800 merchant ships in service currently. Greece has one of the largest merchant shipping fleets in the world. Aristotle Onassis and Stavros Niarchos ("The Golden Greek") are some of the best-known Greek shipping businessmen.

When the Roman Empire split in two in A.D. 285 the eastern half, including Greece, became known as the Byzantine Empire. In 1453, Greece fell to the Ottoman Empire. Greece wouldn't then achieve independence until 1829.

The Electricity supply in Greece is 220 volts AC, 50Hz. Round two-pin plugs are used. North American visitors require a transformer and British visitors an adaptor.

The time in Greece is like most other counties in Europe, Summer (Daylight-Saving) Time is observed in Greece, where the time is shifted forward by 1 hour; 3 hours ahead of Greenwich Mean Time (GMT+3). After the summer months the time in Greece is shifted back by 1 hour to Eastern European Time (EET) or (GMT+2). In Greece the working hours of Banks and Public Services are from 08.00 to 14.00, Monday to Friday. Shops are usually open Monday-Wednesday- Saturday from 09.00 to 15.00 and Tuesday-Thursday-Friday from 09.00 to 14.00 and 17.00 to 20.00. In these three days of the week, shops close for the siesta at noon and open again in the afternoon. In the tourist areas in high season, most shops stay open all day long, from early in the morning till late in the evening. Shopping malls in the cities also stay open all day...

Understanding Greek Traditions

Driving in Greece for those of you that have already sampled the delights of driving on Greek roads you will be familiar with the sometimes unfinished state of the road surface and of the sides of the road and ditches being full of builder's rubble and litter. Beside many of the main roads you will see large advertising boards touting brands of cigarettes, coffee or other goods.

Greek time in the summertime is two hours ahead of the time in the UK (Greenwich meridian time) like elsewhere in Europe. Also in Greece, in the summer season (March – September) you will find that there is something very curious about time. In Greece it is conceived in a very particular way. Here time is not running, there is no such concept of "being on time or late" and a watch is just something to wear. The Greeks themselves are aware of the need for them to take it easy (but not in serving the tourist!) up to the point that G.M.T. is not considered as the Greenwich Meridian Time, but as the Greek Maybe Time! So remember you are on holiday take your time and relax things will get done in the fullness of time or should I say in Greek time.

Religious festivals in Greece have become the true backbone in many communities. All kinds of festivals and religious feast events take place for example Christian Holy events during Easter, when churches are decorated with colourful flowers and bay leaves. The rosary that most of the Greek men are holding in their hands, sitting outside the kafeneion (cafe in Greece), has no religious meaning, but is only a way of killing time. Try and buy one, it's actually much more difficult to swing it than it looks.

On most Greek beaches you will have to pay for a sun bed and an umbrella. If you think that it is just people trying to get money out of the tourists you're very wrong. Having a piece of a beach is a job in Greece. A man bids for a particular part of the beach each year, and he pays a sum of money, to be allowed to put up his sun beds and umbrellas…

The Greek Olive tree trunks are often painted white (lime-wash) in Greece. It is used primarily to fight ants and besides it looks nice, too…

Understanding Greek Traditions

Unfinished buildings is a common sight in Greece. The reason is that Greek people build what they need today and leave the rest of the building unfinished for the future. It may seem that the Greeks are constantly building houses - and they are. Most Greek parents build a house for each daughter, but not for their sons (as they are supposed to marry a girl who will get a house from her parents). Often it is also the daughter that inherits her parents' or grandparents' house when they die. The iron bars sticking out from the flat Greek house roof are exclusively there for the purpose of a later extension to the house. They have, in fact, **NOTHING** to do with exemptions from taxpaying, as long as the house isn't yet finished some people say. (But it is a good story though)!

Greeks in tavernas is a common sight you might think. People may think that Greek men are always sitting in tavernas or cafes drinking. In fact they do often go to a kafeneion, but not always, and rarely for a very long time. Often they have a cup of Greek coffee only. Most of them stay there for a short time, just enough to hear what has happened and also to make an appointment with for example the local electrician or the local bricklayer. Of course, Greek women can go to the kafeneion as well, but most of them don't want to, and besides they hear all the gossip from the husband when he comes home. For about 20 years ago, you would always find at least two kafenions in a village, no matter how small it was, but painted in different colours. The colours indicated the political party of the owner of the kafenion. This way you avoided political quarrels. Rather practical! It can still be found, but it has become more and more rare as less and less people care about politics in Greece today.

Theft in Greece is very, very rare. It's simply considered too humiliating to steel other people's things or money. On the other hand it's OK to cheat a bit - especially if they don't like the person that they cheat.

A Greek priest - or pappas as they are called are everywhere, as you cannot miss them in their long, black dress and high hat. They are not obliged to wear their priest clothes all the time, but they do, as it is most practical and they are easier to identify this way. Greek priests can marry and have children, just like in the Lutheran church. But you will never see a woman priest. This is not allowed by the Greek Orthodox Church…

Understanding Greek Traditions

Getting dressed up ready for church in Greece. If you want to see a Greek Church or monastery inside, you must be properly dressed. It's considered rude to enter a church if your shoulders and knees aren't covered. This rule goes for both men and women. So if you are a tourist and wants to be polite in the country you are visiting then please dress respectfully when visiting one of their churches.

Getting a Greek invitation. If a Greek invites you out for dinner or a drink, don't **EVER** try to make him "split the bill in half" as we often do here in the UK. If you do the Greek man will be more embarrassed than you could ever imagine! If you are invited to a Greeks home, remember to bring something for the hosts. Flowers or chocolate is the most common. If the occasion is a name day, you must bring a present, which you deliver when you enter the house. The present will be put together with the rest of the presents on a table - unopened. The Greeks will open the gifts when all the guests have left. If he or she doesn't like the gift they don't have to pretend or show a lot of gratitude that they do not feel. Actually this is a very practical habit.

Officially there is equality between the sexes but still in Greece today, as in the UK, women are often paid less. About 40 % of the Greek women are engaged in active employment. Theoretically Greek women are liable for military service, but only volunteers are enlisted and the women seem to be satisfied with this situation. In Greece when divorcing, all belongings are equally split between the man and woman. A Greek woman may keep her maiden name when marrying. The Greek birth-rate is the second lowest in Europe. Italy has the lowest birth-rate. In Greece since 1982 it has been legal to have a civil marriage. But still 95 % are married religiously in the church. In Greece arranged marriages are forbidden by law. Paying dowry is also illegal too. But today you can still find examples of both especially in the villages…

Understanding Greek Traditions

Bullet holes in road signs. It is no secret that Greeks own guns, especially in mountainous areas. Therefore, road signs are easy targets and you will see many of them that resemble Swiss cheese after suffering from some shooting practice. Greeks also usually fire their guns at weddings and other celebrations.

Greek churches (ekklisies). Large churches are usually found inside the towns but the numerous small ones are practically everywhere. Usually they are white-painted, you will find them on a beach, on the mountain peaks, in deep gorges or inside caves. The people of Greece are deeply religious people and they build churches to express their gratitude to God or to fulfil a "tama", a promise given to God in exchange for a request. The miniature churches next to the roads however, are memorials for people killed or injured in a car accidents, they are at the same spot where the accident happened. The family of the deceased construct and maintains the shine. They usually contain a photo of the deceased, some religious objects and a lit candle.

Greek herb. Erontas or diktamos is the Greek name for the herb dittany: It used to be a rare, hard to collect herb because it grew on steep cliffs in mountainous areas. Today it is cultivated, so it has become easy to find. It is said that its name "erontas", which is actually the same word as erotas, was given to it because a man should be deeply in love with a woman in order to risk his life to collect it for her from a steep cliff. Fresh fish in Greece has become rare and quite expensive. Common fish that you will find at restaurants are: red mullet, sea bream, red snapper, swordfish and tuna. octopus, squids, shrimps and mussels are also easy to find and they taste great. Fish like Sand-Smelt or Silverside are quite cheap and tasty, although its taste is described as "fishy" by people who are not used to Mediterranean fish. Garides are shrimps and you can have them grilled, boiled or "saganaki" with tomatoes and feta cheese…

Understanding Greek Traditions

Greek Salad. In Greek it is called "horiatiki" and it is a tasty salad made from fresh tomatoes, cucumber, olives and feta cheese. Add some oregano, vinegar and plenty of Greek olive oil and you have a tasty and fulfilling dish. Greek herbs: If I had to describe Greece in just five words only, then I would choose: sun, sea, mountains, sage and thyme. Sage and thyme are everywhere in Greece and the air is full of their characteristic smell. Herbs have been used for ages by the people of Greece as medicines. Try a tea of camomile and sage if you have a sore throat. If you do not like the taste you can add some honey to it. If your nose is blocked and you cannot breathe easily, then have a tea made from thyme. Greek honey: Honey of excellent quality is produced in Greece. Thyme honey is considered to be the best. Lamb meat: The best meat you can have in Greece is the young lamb or young goat meat from animals raised in the mountainous areas. If you happen to be in a taverna in a small mountainous village, ask them for grilled paidakia. Mizithra: Is a fresh soft white cheese. It contains lower fat and cholesterol than yellow cheese is made from sheep's milk. Paximadi: Is the traditional Greek way of preserving bread for a long time. It is hard dried bread that gets soft when you add some water to it. You will find it in various forms, sizes and made from wheat or barley, with or without yeast, whole grain or not. Pour some olive oil on a big round piece of paximadi, add some grated tomato, oregano and feta cheese and you will have the very tasty appetizer. Pita Giros: Are slices of grilled pork meat with yoghurt, lots of onion, French fries, salt and pepper, all wrapped inside a round "pita" bread. Pita - giros is the fast food of Greece and you can find it almost everywhere. Chicken giros is becoming popular lately because of the smaller amount of fat that it contains.

Non-Greeks. Immigrants such as Albanians, Bulgarians, Russians, Ukranian and others from Eastern Europe have moved to Greece in big numbers over the years. Most of them work in agriculture and construction and their number is now more than 10% of the Greek population. They adjusted quickly to the Greek way of life and their children go to Greek schools...

Understanding Greek Traditions

Sariki. Is the traditional head covering for the men of Crete. It is black and is wrapped many times around the top of the head.

Souvlaki. Is skewered pork meat, a traditional Greek dish. It is usually served with French fries and there is also chicken, lamb and swordfish souvlaki. Greek Vegetables: Greece produces many different kinds of vegetables and they taste a lot better than what you will find in the supermarkets in the rest of Europe.

Xanthies. Are blonde tourist women. Highly appreciated by the "kamakia", the young hot-blooded Greek lovers. Love stories between the men of Greece and female tourists are common every year. Most of them are just summer love but a few marriages do come out of them. The result is that there are many European women living in Greece, mostly German, Dutch and Scandinavian. Be aware though, that having a romantic love affair during your holiday is one thing and living in Greece married to a Greek man is totally another. The cultural differences are many and it is important not to ignore them.

Yannis and Yorgos. Are the two most common names for men in Greece. Yannis is John and Yorgos is George. More common names are Manolis and Nikos. For women the most common name is Maria.

Having now read about the culture and traditions of the people of Greece it is now time for us, in the next chapter , to enjoy the beautiful paradise Greek Island of Skiathos in Colour…

Skiathos in Colour

Pictures of a Greek Paradise

Skiathos in Colour

Pictures of a Greek Paradise

Skiathos in Colour

Pictures of a Greek Paradise

Skiathos in Colour

Pictures of a Greek Paradise

Skiathos in Colour

Pictures of a Greek Paradise

Skiathos in Colour

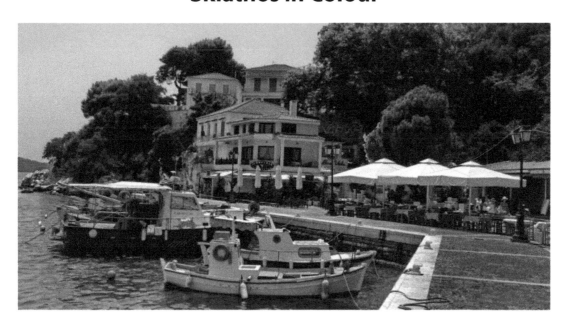

Pictures of a Greek Paradise

Skiathos in Colour

Pictures of a Greek Paradise

Skiathos in Colour

Pictures of a Greek Paradise

Skiathos in Colour

Pictures of a Greek Paradise

Skiathos in Colour

Pictures of a Greek Paradise

Skiathos in Colour

Pictures of a Greek Paradise

Skiathos in Colour

Pictures of a Greek Paradise

Skiathos in Colour

Pictures of a Greek Paradise

Skiathos in Colour

Pictures of a Greek Paradise

Skiathos in Colour

Pictures of a Greek Paradise

Skiathos in Colour

Pictures of a Greek Paradise

Skiathos in Colour

Pictures of a Greek Paradise

Skiathos in Colour

Pictures of a Greek Paradise

Skiathos in Colour

Pictures of a Greek Paradise

Skiathos in Colour

Pictures of a Greek Paradise

Skiathos in Colour

Pictures of a Greek Paradise

Skiathos in Colour

TROULOS BAY HOTEL TEAM - SKIATHOS

Pictures of a Greek Paradise

Skiathos in Colour

Pictures of a Greek Paradise

Skiathos in Colour

Pictures of a Greek Paradise

Skiathos in Colour

Pictures of a Greek Paradise

Skiathos in Colour

Pictures of a Greek Paradise

Skiathos in Colour

Pictures of a Greek Paradise

Skiathos in Colour

Pictures of a Greek Paradise

Skiathos in Colour

Pictures of a Greek Paradise

Skiathos in Colour

Pictures of a Greek Paradise

Skiathos in Colour

Pictures of a Greek Paradise

Skiathos in Colour

Pictures of a Greek Paradise

Skiathos in Colour

Pictures of a Greek Paradise

Skiathos in Colour

Pictures of a Greek Paradise

Skiathos in Colour

Pictures of a Greek Paradise

Skiathos in Colour

Pictures of a Greek Paradise

Skiathos in Colour

Pictures of a Greek Paradise

Skiathos in Colour

Pictures of a Greek Paradise

Skiathos in Colour

Above is a scene of people watching a plane as it lands, with holidaymakers on, coming to enjoy their summer holiday on the paradise Greek Island of Skiathos. If the people stay a little while they may see the same plane as it takes off again laden with some other people on their way back home at the end of their holiday. We too are about to do just that in the last chapter of this book as Susie and I prepare to leave the island of our dreams, the place we love the Island of Skiathos behind us!...

Leaving Paradise

Going Home...

The Skiathos airport departure hall and a plane ready to leave paradise

It is amazing how time fly's especially when you are on holiday. One day you are unpacking your cases and it seems that in a blink of an eye you are re-packing them again! I know that it is the same for us all but why is it always over so quick! Like many, we always try to squeeze as much into our holiday as we can but still it is always sad to have to leave again! On the day we are due to fly home Susie and I always spend a couple of hours on the beach swimming and sunbathing first thing in the morning. This done we go up to our room to pack our cases before having a nice refreshing shower. Once we have done this, sat on the balcony for a few minutes before we take our cases down to reception. This done we go into the hotel restaurant (we have to be out of our room by 1 pm by the way) for lunch. After lunch we say our fond farewell to all our holiday friends and the wonderful hotel staff before we catch the tour operators coach to the airport at about 3.45 pm. Upon our arrival at the departure building we collect our cases from the coach driver, enter the departure hall, go through passport control and into the waiting area before boarding our plane at about 7 pm for our flight back to Gatwick airport in the UK...

Leaving Paradise

Alan and a plane getting ready to go down the runway

I should say that before we go into the departure lounge there is often time to have a brief wander around outside. Susie took the above picture of Alan sitting just outside the airport runway perimeter just before it was unfortunately time for us to leave on our plane back to the UK in 2014. All to soon it was time to get on our plane, sit down just before the engine roared, the wheels went up and away we sadly went back home!…

Leaving Paradise

Flyby and a rainbow

As we sit on the plane in our seats there is a tear in our eyes and a rainbow in our hearts as we charge down the runway and into the air and away from our paradise island of Skiathos once more. After a good flight we arrive back in the UK at about 8.20 pm, go through customs, collect our cases and then it's time to retrieve our car and drive home. We arrive back home usually by about mid-night. We are obviously very tired at this point but as we reflect on our holiday and say goodbye to our paradise island we leave you above with one of the great sights of our holiday. This was a rainbow over the Troulos Bay Hotel on our paradise island of Skiathos…

Leaving Paradise

Now that we have come to the end of our story and hopefully enjoyed the rainbow on the previous page and the Skiathan sunset featured above I hope that you now see why we think that Skiathos is truly a paradise island. If you have not been to Skiathos as yet: **WHY NOT!** I am sure that if you do go you will find it well worthwhile. I believe that if you do go and are able to sit and look out at such wonderful sea views and magnificent sunsets that we have enjoyed in this book then I think, like us, who knows, Skiathos may become your Paradise Island too. I hope that you have enjoyed our journey together to this wonderful land and it just leaves me with just one last thing left to say to you my reader and that you will find on the next page…

Leaving Paradise

"The END is nigh"

Well, we have completed our journey safely together around the Greek paradise island of Skiathos. I hope that you have enjoyed the trip. My hope is that our family, our friends and anyone else who reads this book will treasure it, keep it safe and revisit it from time to time or better still go and visit Skiathos for themselves.

We wish you "Happy Holidays" and so until the next time.

Best Wishes from Susie and Alan

Acknowledgement

To all of my family, friends and Skiathan's mentioned or illustrated in this book that have all enriched my life immeasurably, I wish to express my gratitude. I would also like to thank my publishers, Rainbow Publications UK, for giving me the opportunity for my words to be read once more. Finally I wish to thank my wife Susie, for being with me every step of the way. Her love and support inspires me every single day of my life.

It is sadly time to say goodbye until the next time - Yammas (Cheers)